Today's Best Baby Names

Today's Best Baby Names

Alfred J. Kolatch

A Perigee Book

Perigee Books
are published by
The Putnam Publishing Group
200 Madison Avenue
New York, NY 10016

Library of Congress Cataloging-in-Publication Data

Kolatch, Alfred J., date.
    Today's best baby names.

    "A Perigee book."
    Some names and introductory material taken from the au-
thor's Jonathan David dictionary of first names.
        1. Names, Personal—Dictionaries.   I. Kolatch, Alfred J.,
date. Jonathan David dictionary of first names.   II. Title.
CS2367.K653   1986   929.4'4.0321   86-15137
ISBN 0-399-51271-3

Book design by The Sarabande Press

Typeset by Fisher Composition, Inc.

Printed in the United States of America

        2   3   4   5   6   7   8   9   10

Today's Best Baby Names

Introduction

Where Do Our Names Come From?

OLD TESTAMENT NAMES

The earliest personal names on record are found in the Bible. Many are still in use in their original form and some names, like Rachel, Adam and Sara are very popular today. For the most part, biblical names are easy to understand because their roots are easily traced, usually to the Hebrew; in fact, many are explained in the Bible itself.

The Hebrew root of the name Cain, for example, is *kanoh*, meaning "to acquire, to buy." The verse in Genesis (4:1) explains it: "And she [Eve] conceived and bore Cain, and said, "I have *acquired* a man [Cain] with the help of the Lord."

Adam and Eve's third son was named Seth. In Genesis (4:25), Eve says, "For God has given me another seed [child] instead of Abel; for Cain slew him." The name of this child, Seth [Shes], in Hebrew, has the meaning "to give, to put, to appoint."

Scores of such examples can be found in the pages of the Bible. Clearly, names given to offspring were usually derived directly from the personal lives and experiences of parents.

CHRISTIAN NAMES

Christians of the first centuries used Old Testament Hebrew names. In time, however, these were abandoned by many New Testament figures as a form of protest against Judaism. Thus, the man once known as Simon bar Jonah came to be called Peter, and Saul of Tarsus became known as Paul.

During those early centuries many Christian parents followed the pattern of choosing names associated with mythology and idolatry, even though they abhorred both. Phoebe, Olympius, and Jovianus were commonly used.

THE REFORMATION

Not until the Reformation, in the 1500s, when as a rebellion against the Catholic church and its authority Protestantism came into being, did biblical names—particularly Old Testament names—again become popular. In seventeenth-century Puritan England, where the Reformation turned into a crusade against all church dogma and ceremonials, New Testament names in particular were renounced in favor of Old Testament names.

Many Puritan extremists, even those living as late as the eighteenth and nineteenth centuries, went so far as to use the most obscure and odd-sounding names they could find; they even took phrases from Scripture and used them—in their entirety—as names. Ernest Weekley, in his book *Jack and Jill,* reports that at the beginning of the twentieth century there was a family with the names Asenath Zaphnath Paaneah, Kezia Jemima Keren Happukh, and Maher Shalal Hashbaz.

Additional strange appellations used by Puritans include Free-gift, Reformation, Earth, Dust, Ashes, Delivery, Morefruit, Tribulation, The Lord Is Near, More Trial, Discipline, and Joy Again. One Puritan parent named his child If-Christ-had-not-died-for-you-you-had-been-damned-bare-bones, but his acquaintances, becoming weary of its length, retained only the last part, Damned-Barebones. The average Puritan, however, was satisfied with Old Testament names as well as those derived from abstract virtues, such as Perseverance, Faith, Hope, Humility, Charity, and Repentance. A pair of twin girls born to the English Wycliffe family in 1710 were named Favour and Fortune.

The Quakers (Society of Friends), like the Puritans, preferred Old Testament names and despised the nomenclature of the New Testament, probably as part of their protest against the Church of England, with whom they broke in 1648. The Quakers disapproved of the elaborate ceremonies of the established church.

NAMES FROM PLACES

Many first names, like surnames, have been borrowed from the names of places. Here are a few examples which have been submitted by our correspondents:

- *Mrs. O. K. Hauch, Houston, Texas:* "My great-grandfather named his daughters after states he had visited: Ohio, Virginia, Nebraska, Indiana."
- *Kimberley Worthington, Chattanooga, Tennessee:* "In 1949 my mother was visiting her father in Cape Town, South Africa, and was taken on a tour of the great Kimberley Diamond Mine. She was impressed with the name and promised herself that she would name her daughter Kimberley."
- *Alsace Lorraine Stewart, Conroe, Texas:* "My daddy—now nearing ninety years of age— was a foot soldier during World War I. In 1917, while in Germany in Alsace Lorraine,

he became ill from the effects of mustard gas. He recovered and was grateful! I was born on June 14, 1921, and my mother and daddy named me Alsace Lorraine."

NATURE NAMES

Nature has always been a prime source for our nomenclature. The Bible abounds in such names, as does the mythology of all early peoples. The practice continues to this day. Here are some samples submitted by our correspondents:

- *Silver A. Kim, Pleasanton, California:* "My Mom told me she often watched the wind blow the leaves on a silver maple tree that she had planted in our backyard. She said they looked so beautiful blowing in the wind that she would name her next daughter Silver."
- *Sunny Jean Bond, Red Bluff, California:* "My name is Sunny Jean (married name Bond). My first name came about because my mother said to Sister Superior at the hospital, 'No matter whether a boy or a girl, the first name will be Sunny because for the first time in days the sun was shining.'"
- *Karen Shannon, Pacifica, California:* "[My daughter] Dandylyon Rosebud Shannon was conceived in a large field of dandelions in a small town in New Mexico. It seemed only proper and fitting to name her after the flower she bloomed from."

CALENDAR NAMES

In the course of history we find that a great many of the days of the week, months of the year, and holidays have constituted a source of first names as well as surnames. Monday (spelled Munday), Tuesday (Dienstag, in German), and Saturday were commonly used as names. Friday, the famous character in *Robinson Crusoe*, is well known to all.

Although many of the months of the year have been used as surnames, they have been used to a greater extent as first names. Augustus (August) and Julia (July) were especially common in Roman days. April, May and June are occasionally encountered today. Howard Fast, in his book *Patrick Henry and the Frigate's Keel*, records the name of January Fernandez, a Portuguese who participated in the breaking of the British blockade in 1812.

Among the Christian holidays, Easter and Christmas have long served as sources for forenames. Easter is commonly used and can be found as a character in Lillian Smith's novel *Strange Fruit*, and Christ and Christmas are the backbone of names such as Chris, Christopher, Christine, and Noel.

NUMERAL NAMES

Numbers are another source for names that were used a great deal in the past and are used in some rare instances today. The Romans were the first to take numeral names. Among the more common are Quintus (5), Octavius (8), and Septimus (7). There was recently a family in Michigan by the surname Stickaway that named their three boys One, Two, and Three; and their three girls, First, Second, and Third.

One of our correspondents, Joyce Pagan of Gilroy, California, writes: "My mother was to be named Mabel, but a friend of her parents offered to buy her first pair of shoes if they would name her Nina (for "nine"). The reason: she was born on the nineteenth day of the ninth month of the year nineteen nineteen at nine A.M."

OCCUPATIONAL NAMES

Many occupational names have become first names, although the vast majority have come down to us as last names. Most fall into the category of the name Wright, which is an Old English name meaning "an artisan, a worker." It is used occasionally as a first name (e.g., Wright Morris, the author), but for the most part it has remained a surname (e.g., the Wright brothers, Orville and Wilbur).

Middle English names were often occupational names. Bannister, meaning "one who draws a crossbow," and Brewster, meaning "one who brews beer," are used from time to time. Newly created names are rarely based on occupation.

PERSONAL PREFERENCES

A large group of names has come into being for no reason other than a mother- or father-to-be took a liking to a certain sound or was overcome by a sudden inspiration. In some cases the name was selected as a lark.

Bill Lear, a radio executive in the 1940s, named his daughter Chrystal Chanda Lear (chandelier).

Charles Fisher, in his book *The Columnist*, reports that Walter Winchell's wife wanted to call their child Reid (read) Winchell if it were a boy, while he preferred Sue Winchell in the event the offspring were a girl. Ben Bernie, who at the time was carrying on a prearranged feud with Winchell, suggested the name Lynch Winchell. In the end the boy was named Walter, Jr., but Winchell's daughter, who was born some nine years earlier, was named Walda, and was undoubtedly so named because it sounded very much like Walter.

Here are a few examples submitted by our correspondents:

- *Verena Shubert, Hidden Hills, California:* "My name is Verena. My mother was also named Verena. Her mother took the F off of Ferena cereal and put a V in the place of F."
- *Candy Martin, Mannington, West Virginia:* "A good friend of mine is a teacher. She has two new students this year, one named Rusty Irons and the other Penny Coin."
- *Jacqui Moore, Vacaville, California:* "In 1968 a television commercial for an aftershave lotion mentioned the name Joelle. That was it. We named our daughter Joelle, and Joey is her nickname. A few years later I discovered when visiting my hometown that one of my friends gave her daughter the same name. She had seen the same commercial!"

HYBRID AND SCRAMBLED NAMES

A considerable number of new names are newly coined names created by parents or grandparents who want to preserve part of an old name. Therefore, they scramble the letters of a name to create a new one, or they join parts of two or more names to accomplish the same purpose. We include in this category of newly coined names acronyms, which are formed by combining the first letters of several words or names.

Our correspondents have shared with us a large sampling of such name creations:

- *Pia Lindstrom,* the television newscaster and daughter of Dr. Peter Aron Lindstrom and actress Ingrid Bergman, advises us that her name is a combination of *P*eter, *I*ngrid, and *A*ron.
- *Graylen Milligan, Webster, New York:* "When my parents adopted me, they wanted me to be uniquely theirs, to always feel part of

them. They decided to do this by giving me a name derived from theirs. My father was Graydon and my mother Helen. I was named Graylen."

· *Kathy Blagrone, Maybrook, New York:* "My daughter, Kaela Janelle, was named for four people: KAthy (mother), LArry (father), JANet (a friend), ELLa (grandmother). The "e" was added to the first and the middle name."

· *Sister Joel Read, Milwaukee, Wisconsin:* "My father's name was Joseph and my mother's name was Ellen. The first two letters of both names were joined and I was named Joel."

· *Nira Lynn Dolan, Livonia, Michigan:* "My name, Nira, is an acronym my grandmother made up from the National Industrial Recovery Act."

CELEBRITY NAMES

Many of our names today, as in the past, have been adopted because they were the names of celebrities or centered about events in the lives of celebrities. In this category we include not only contemporary celebrities in the fields of entertainment, sports, music, politics, etc., but also the great figures of history, political as well as religious, whose charisma was so great that parents named children after them.

When Alexander the Great entered Palestine in 333 B.C., according to the legend, all Jewish boys born in that year were named Alexander in his honor.

Hugh, originally spelled Hew, became a popular name in England after the thirteenth century because of the popularity of Hugh of Lincoln, an infant-martyr. After he was canonized by the Catholic church, his name became even more popular and gave rise to many surnames, such as Uet, Hutchins, Higgins, and Hughes.

Introduction

Many Catholics are named after saints. Among the most popular is Saint Patrick (c. 387-463), whose name is often bestowed on babies born in March, particularly those born on March 17, the feast day assigned by the church to commemorate his life.

Protestants sometimes choose a famous or well-liked minister as a namesake. One can hardly doubt that the name of Luther Martin, a delegate from Maryland to the Constitutional Convention in Philadelphia, was inspired by Martin Luther. In *Get Thee Behind Me,* author Hartzell Spence tells that he was named after Bishop Hartzell.

Inspired by the peace treaty between Israel and Egypt signed in Washington, D.C., in March 1979, Mr. and Mrs. Hotam El Kabassi named their triplets born on April 5, 1979, Carter, Begin, and Sadat in honor of U.S. President Jimmy Carter, Israeli Prime Minister Menachem Begin, and Egyptian President Anwar Sadat, the three principals at the signing.

Our correspondents have provided us with a wide variety of examples that fall into this category:

- *Yvonne Abner, Blanchester, Ohio:* "My name is Yvonne Deniese Abner (nee Coogan). My initials are Y.D.C., and I was named after Yvonne DeCarlo."
- *Cassandra M. Sherod, Honolulu, Hawaii:* "My daughter is of Irish, Scotch, and Japanese descent. At the time of my pregnancy I attended a movie which starred a famous Irish actress named Siobhan McKenna. I heard the name pronounced as Shevon, and it seemed to go nicely with our last name. My daughter was named Shevon Sherod."
- *Nancy Reece Darby, San Diego, California:* "My father was a member of the U.S. Army band playing trombone and trumpet. Frank Sinatra had a new song out—'Nancy With the Laughing Face'—about his daughter. It was my father's favorite song. When he

found out his first child was a girl, he decided to name me after that favorite song."

UNCONVENTIONAL SPELLINGS

For the past two or three decades many new first names have come into being as a result of a desire on the part of parents to be different or distinctive. They have increasingly been taking popular names and spelling them differently.

The most common characteristic of this new fad is substituting a "y" for an "i" or adding an "e." Fannye was once Fannie, and Mollye was formerly Mollie. Likewise, Sadie has become Sadye, and Edith has become Edyth or Edythe. Shirley has become Shirlee, Shirlie, or Sherle. Sarah and Hannah have dropped the "h" and become Sara and Hanna. Esther can now be found as Ester and sometimes as Esta or Estee.

Among the many feminine names that have, because of a new spelling, made their appearance of late, are the following familiar ones: Rosalin, Rosaline, Rosalyn, Roselyn, Roslyn, Roslyne, and Rosylin from Rosalind; Debra and Dobra from Deborah; Karolyn and Carolyn from Caroline; Alyce and Alyse from Alice; Gale from Gail; Arlyne from Arline; Arleyne from Arlene; Lilyan from Lilian; Elane and Elayne from Elaine; Ilene and Iline from Eileen; Ethyl and Ethyle from Ethel; Janis from Janice; Jayne from Jane; Madeline, Madelon, Madelyn, Madelyne, and Madlyn from Madeleine; Marilin and Marylin from Marilyn; and Vyvyan and Vivien from Vivian.

Changes in spelling also account for a large number of new masculine names. Prominent among these are: Allan, Alyn, Allyn, and Allen from Alan; Frederic, Fredric, and Fredrick from Frederick; Irwin, Erwin, Irving, and Irvine from Irvin; Isidore, Isador, and Isadore from Isidor; Laurance, Laurence, Lawrance, and Lorence from

Lawrence; Maury, Morey, and Morry from Morris; Murry from Murray; and Mervyn from Mervin.

MASCULINE/FEMININE INTERCHANGES

A substantial number of names in contemporary use have been "borrowed" from the opposite sex, sometimes without modification, but usually after a slight change has been made.

Among women's names we find a vast number adopted from the masculine forms. In many instances, the feminine name is so long established and accepted that we no longer realize that it had its origin in a masculine name. In this group the following are prominent: Alexandra and Alexandria from Alexander; Charlotte and Charleene from Charles; Davi, Davida, and Davita from David; Erica from Eric; Frederica from Frederic; Georgia, Georgine, and Georgette from George; Harriet and Harri from Harry; Henrietta, Henri, and Henria from Henry; Herma and Hermine from Herman; Horatio (daughter of Horatio "Lord" Nelson and Lady Hamilton) from Horatio; Isaaca from Isaac; Josepha and Josephine from Joseph; Lou, Louise, and Louisa from Louis (the wife of Herbert Hoover was Lou Henry Hoover); Roberta from Robert; Stephanie from Stephan; and Willa and Willene from Will or William. Other less common feminine names of masculine origin are Alexis, Alwyn, Barnetta, Cary, Ellys, Franklyne, Freddie, Herberta, Jamie, Joelle, Merril, Merrill, Meryl, Raymonde, Roye, Simona, Simonne, and Toni.

This list is long and can be supplemented with many additional names found in this dictionary.

PET FORMS (DIMINUTIVES)

Pet forms, often called diminutives (although, this is not a precise characterization of the form), make up a large portion of our contemporary first names. This group grows larger and larger as the desire for self expression grows stronger. Often, the original Christian, baptismal first name of an individual is completely abandoned and the pet name becomes the real name.

The most common form of the pet name has evolved by dropping the last letter or syllable of the original name and adding to it "y" or "ie" or "ette."

Masculine
Names

A

Aaron From a variety of Hebrew roots, meaning "to sing," "to shine," "to teach," or "a mountain." Also, from the Arabic, meaning "a messenger."

Abbe, Abbey, Abby From the Old French *abaie* and the Late Latin *abbatia*, meaning "the head of a monastery, an abbot."

Abbot, Abott Derived from Abba, meaning "father."

Abel From the Hebrew *hevel*, meaning "a breath" or "vapor."

Abraham From the Hebrew, meaning "father of a multitude."

Abram From the Hebrew, meaning "father of might" or "exalted father." The original name of Abraham.

Ace From the Latin *as* and the Middle English *aas*, meaning "a unit, unity."

Adam From the Hebrew *adamah*, meaning "earth."

Addison   Old English patronymic form of Adam, meaning "the son of Adam."

Adler   From the German, meaning "eagle."

Adolph   From the Old German, compounded of *athal,* meaning "noble," and *wolfa,* meaning "wolf." In Old English, Aethelwulf was the form used until the eleventh century. Adolphe is the French form.

Adrian   A short form of the Latin name Hadrian.

Adriel   From the Hebrew, meaning "God is my majesty." In the Bible, King Saul's son-in-law.

Ainsley   From the Scotch, meaning "one's own meadow, one's own field."

Al   A pet name for many first names: Albert, Alfred, Alexander, etc.

Alan   From the Middle Latin name Alanus.

Alastair   A Gaelic form of Alexander.

Albert   A French form of the Old High German name Adelbrecht. Albert is compounded of the Old High German *adal,* meaning "noble, nobility," and *beraht,* meaning "bright."

Alberti, Alberto   Italian forms of Albert.

Alcot, Alcott   From the Old English, meaning "old cottage."

Alden   From the Middle English *elde,* meaning "old age, antiquity."

Aldon   A variant spelling of Alden.

Alec, Aleck Short forms of Alexander, popular in Scotland.

Alexander From the Greek name Alexandros, meaning "protector of men."

Alexis A variant form of Alexander. Used also as a feminine name.

Alfred From the Old English *aelf*, meaning "elf" (and having the connotation of wise, clever), and *raed*, meaning "counsel."

Alger From the Anglo-Saxon, meaning "noble spear, noble warrior."

Ali A form of Allah, the Supreme Being of the Mohammedan religion.

Alic, Alick Variant forms of Alex, a pet form of Alexander popular in Scotland.

Alistair, Allistair, Allister Variant spellings of Alastair.

Allan Variant spelling of Alan.

Allen The more common spelling of Allan.

Allston From the Old English, meaning "Al's (elf's) town."

Alphonso From the Old High German *athal* and *adal*, meaning "noble," plus the Latin *funds*, meaning "estate"; hence "nobleman's estate."

Alvan From the Latin *albus*, meaning "white," or from the Old High German, meaning "old friend" or "noble friend."

Alvin A variant form of Alvan.

Alwin, Alwyn   From the Old English, meaning "noble friend" or "elf friend." Akin to Alvan or Alvin.

Amado   A variant form of Amadeus, meaning "love of God."

Amal   From the Hebrew, meaning "work, toil."

Anastasius   From the Greek, meaning "resurrection."

Amos   From the Hebrew, meaning "to be burdened, troubled."

Anatole, Anatoly   From the Greek, meaning "rising of the sun," or "from the east."

Andre, Andres   The French and Spanish forms of Andrew.

Andreas   The Latin form of Andrew.

Andrew   From the Greek, meaning "manly, valiant, courageous."

Andros   A Greek form of Andrew.

Andy   A pet form of Andrew.

Angelo   An Italian form of Angel, from the Greek, meaning "a messenger or saintly person."

Angus   From the Gaelic and Irish, meaning "exceptional, outstanding."

Anson, Ansonia   From the Anglo-Saxon, meaning "the son of Ann" or "the son of Hans."

Anton, Antone, Antonin   Variant forms of Antony.

Antonino   A variant form of Anthony.

Antonio   The Italian, Spanish, and Portuguese form of Antony.

Antony, Anthony   From the Greek, meaning "flourishing," and from the Latin, meaning "worthy of praise." Antonius is the original form.

Anwar   From the Arabic, meaning "light."

Aram   From the Assyrian *aramu*, meaning "high, heights." The ancient name of Syria, whose language was Aramaic.

Arch   A short form of Archibald. Also used as an independent name.

Archibald   From the Anglo-Saxon, meaning "very bold" or "holy prince."

Ardon   From the Hebrew, meaning "bronze."

Arel   From the Hebrew, meaning "lion of God." Ariel is a variant form.

Ari   From the Hebrew, meaning "a lion."

Aric, Arick   Early German forms of Richard.

Aristo   From the Greek *aristos*, meaning "the best."

Arlee   A variant form of Arleigh or Arles, originally a Hebrew word, *eravon*, meaning "a pledge, a promise to pay."

Arlen   The Celtic form of Arles, meaning "a pledge."

Arley   A variant spelling of Arlee.

Arlo Probably from the Old English, meaning "a fortified hill."

Armand French and Italian form of the Old German name Hermann, meaning "warrior."

Armando A Spanish form of Armand.

Armond A variant spelling of Armand.

Armon From the Hebrew, meaning "castle, palace."

Arnie A pet form of Arnold.

Arno A short form of Arnold.

Arnold From the Old German, compounded from *aran*, meaning "eagle," and *wald*, meaning "power."

Arthur From the Gaelic *art*, meaning "a rock," hence "noble, lofty hill"; or, from the Celtic *artos*, meaning "a bear."

Artro, Arturo Variant forms of Arthur.

Ashley From the Old English, meaning "a field of ash trees."

August A short form of Augustus.

Augustus From the Latin, meaning "revered, exalted."

Austen, Austin English variant forms of August and Augustus.

Avery A variant form of Aubrey, from the Teutonic, meaning "elf ruler."

ℬ

Bailey, Bayley   From the Middle English *bail* and *baile*, meaning "fortification" or "outer castle wall."

Barak   From the Hebrew, meaning "flash of light."

Barclay   A variant form of Berkely, from the Anglo-Saxon, meaning "birch meadow."

Bard   From the Gaelic and Irish, meaning "a minstrel, a poet."

Barden   From the Anglo-Saxon, meaning "a valley where barley grows."

Bardon   A variant of Barden.

Barnabas   From the Latin, Greek, and Aramaic, meaning "son of exhortation."

Barnaby   A variant form of Barnabas.

Barnard   The French form of Bernard.

Barnes   From the Old English *beorna*, meaning "a bear."

Barnet, Barnett   Variant forms of Bernard.

Barney   A pet form of Bernard and Barnaby.

Barret, Barrett   Short forms of Barnett.

Barry   A Welsh patronymic form of Harry (from Ap-Harry and Ab-Harry), meaning "son of Harry."

Bart   A pet form of Barton and Bartholomew.

Bartholomew A patronymic form meaning "son of Talmai."

Bartlett A variant form of Bartholomew.

Bartley From the Anglo-Saxon, meaning "Bart's (Bartholomew's) field."

Barton From the Anglo-Saxon, meaning "Bart's (Bartholomew's) town."

Baxter From the Old English, meaning "a baker."

Baylor From the Anglo-Saxon, meaning "one who trains horses."

Beaumont From the French, meaning "beautiful mountain."

Beauregard From the French, meaning "to be well regarded."

Ben From the Hebrew, meaning "son."

Benedict From the Latin *benedictio*, meaning "to speak well of, to bless."

Benjamin From the Hebrew, meaning "son of my right hand," having the connotation of favoritism.

Bennet, Bennett Variant English forms of the Latin name Benedict.

Benny A pet form of Benjamin.

Benson A patronymic form, meaning "Ben's son."

Bentley, Bently From the Old English *beonot*, meaning "a meadow of ben (grass)."

Benton From the Anglo-Saxon, meaning "Ben's town."

Bernard From the Old High German name Berinhard, meaning "bold as a bear." Bernardo is the Italian and Spanish form.

Berni, Bernie Popular pet forms of Bernard.

Bert, Bertie Pet forms of Albert, Berthold, Bertol, Bertram.

Bertol A variant form of Berthold, from the German, meaning "bright."

Berton A variant form of Bertol.

Bertram From the Old High German *beraht*, meaning "bright, illustrious one."

Berwin From the Anglo-Saxon, meaning "powerful friend."

Bill, Billie, Billy, Billye Variant pet forms of William.

Blaine From the Old English, meaning "the source of a river."

Blair From the Celtic, meaning "a place."

Bo A pet form of Bogart.

Bob, Bobbie, Bobby Pet forms of Robert.

Bogart From the Gaelic *bog* and the Irish *bogach*, meaning "soft, marshy ground."

Booker From the Anglo-Saxon *boc* and *bec*, meaning "beech tree."

Borg From the Old Norse, meaning "a castle." Also, a variant form of the German *berg*, meaning "a mountain."

Boris From the Russian, meaning "to fight."

Bosley From the Old English, meaning "a grove of trees, a thicket."

Boswell From the Old English, meaning "a thicket of willow trees."

Brad A pet form of Braden.

Braden From the Old English, meaning "broad."

Bradford From the Anglo Saxon, meaning "the broad ford."

Bradley From the Old English, meaning "a broad lea, a meadow."

Brady From the Anglo-Saxon, meaning "broad island."

Bram A short form of Abraham or Abram.

Brandon A variant form of Bran, from the Irish, meaning "a raven."

Braxton From the Anglo-Saxon, meaning "Brock's town."

Bret, Brett From the Celtic, meaning "a Breton, a native of Brittany."

Brewster An occupational name. From the Middle English *breuen*, meaning "one who brews or makes beer."

Brian Derived from the Celtic and Gaelic name Briareus, meaning "strong." Bryan, and Bryant are variant forms.

Brindley, Brinley From the Middle English *brended* and *brennen,* meaning "to burn," hence "having a gray or tawny color."

Brit A short form of Briton. An early name for Wales.

Briton, Britton Early forms for Britain. Used by the Celts when they inhabited the British Isles.

Bronson From the Old English, meaning "son of Brown."

Brook, Brooke, Brooks From the Old English *broc,* meaning "a stream." Used also as a feminine name.

Bruce A Scottish form of the French name Brieux, probably meaning "woods."

Bud, Budd From the Anglo-Saxon *budda,* meaning "a beetle," or from the German, meaning "to swell up," as the bud on a branch. Commonly used as a slang expression for a boy or a man.

Buddy A pet form of Bud. In an early British dialect *butty* meant "companion."

Burgess From the Middle English and Old French, meaning "a shopkeeper," hence "a freeman of a borough."

Burley A variant spelling of Burleigh, meaning "a field with knotted tree trunks."

Burnham From the Old English, meaning "the hamlet near the brook."

Burrell   A variant form of Burr, from the Middle English *burre,* meaning "a prickly coating on a plant."

Burt, Burte   Pet forms of Burton.

Burton   From the Old English, meaning "town on a hill."

Byrne   From the Anglo-Saxon, meaning "a coat of armor."

Byron   From the German, meaning "the cottage." Or, from the Old English, meaning "a bear."

C

Cadwell   A variant form of Cadmar and Cadmus, a Welsh name derived from the Greek, meaning "warrior."

Calder   From the Celtic, meaning "from the stony river."

Caldwell   A variant form of Cadwell.

Cale   Possibly a pet form of Caleb, from the Hebrew, meaning "a dog," hence "faithful."

Calhoun   From the Celtic, meaning "a warrior."

Calvin   From the Latin *calvus,* meaning "bald." Cal is a pet form.

Cameron   From the Celtic, meaning "bent nose."

Campbell   Compounded of the Latin *campus,* meaning "a field," and the French *belle,* meaning "beautiful."

Carl A corrupt form of the Old English names Ceorl and Charl, variant forms of Charles.

Carleton A variant spelling of Carlton.

Carlisle From the Anglo-Saxon, meaning "Carl's island."

Carlo, Carlos Italian and Spanish forms of Charles.

Carlson A patronymic form, meaning "son of Carl."

Carlton From the Old English, meaning "Carl's town."

Carmine The Italian form of Carmen, from the Hebrew *carmel,* meaning "vineyard" or "garden."

Carr From the Scandinavian and Old Norse, meaning "marshy land." Kerr is a variant form.

Carrol, Carroll Variant forms of Carl. Used also as a feminine name.

Carson A patronymic, meaning "son of Carr."

Carsten From the Old English, meaning "a stony marsh."

Carter An Old English occupational name, meaning "cart driver."

Carver An Old English occupational name, meaning "a wood carver, a sculptor."

Cary A variant spelling of Carey, from the Welsh or Cornish, meaning "rocky island."

Case From the Old French *casse,* meaning "a chest, a box."

Casey   From the Celtic, meaning "valorous."

Cassidy   From the Celtic, meaning "ingenious."

Chad   From the Celtic, meaning "battle" or "warrior."

Charles   A French form, from the Anglo-Saxon *ceorl* and the English *churl*, meaning "manly, strong" or, literally, "full-grown."

Charlton   A French-German name derived from Charles and meaning "Charles's town."

Chase   From Old French and Middle English, meaning "the hunt."

Chaz   A variant form of Cassius, from the Old Norman French, meaning "a box, a sheath."

Chester   From the Latin, meaning "fortress, camp." Chet is a popular pet form.

Chevy   From the British, meaning "a hunt, a chase." A name derived from the hunting cry *chivy*, in the ballad *Chevy Chase*.

Chip, Chipper   Derived from *Chippeu*, a tribe of Algonquian Indians. *Chip* is the echoic word for the chipping sparrow.

Christian   From the Latin *christianus*, meaning "a Christian."

Christoff   A variant form of Christopher.

Christopher   From the Greek and Latin, meaning "Christ-bearer."

Chuck   A pet form of Charles.

Cid A Spanish name derived from the Arabic *sayyid*, meaning "a lord." The Cid was an eleventh-century Spanish hero and soldier of fortune.

Ciro A pet form of Cicero, from the Latin, meaning "the orator."

Clancy From the Gaelic and Irish *clann*, meaning "offspring, tribe."

Clarence From the Latin *clarus*, meaning "clear, prominent, illustrious."

Clark, Clarke From the Old English, meaning "clergyman; learned man." A clark, or clerk, was originally a member of a clerical order.

Claron A variant form of Clarence.

Clay From the German *klei*, and the Indo-European *glei*, meaning "to stick together."

Clayton A variant form of Clayland.

Clem A pet form of Clement.

Clement From the Latin *clemens*, meaning "gentle, merciful."

Cleveland From the Old English *clif*, meaning "land near the steep bank."

Cliff, Cliffe From the Old English *clif*, meaning "a steep bank."

Clifford From the Old English, meaning "a crossing near the cliff."

Clifton From the Old English, meaning "the town near the cliff."

Clint A pet form of Clinton.

Clinton From the Anglo-Saxon *klint*, meaning "hill," and *tun*, meaning "town," hence "a town on a hill."

Clyde From the Welsh, meaning "heard from afar." Or, from the British, meaning "a warm and sheltered place."

Clydell A variant form of Clyde.

Coburn From the Middle English *burne*, meaning "a little stream," and the prefix *co*, meaning "together," hence "where the streams come together."

Coby A pet form of Coburn.

Cody From the Anglo-Saxon *codd*, akin to the Old Norse *koddi*, meaning "a cushion."

Colbert A French name from the Latin *collum*, meaning "the neck," and the Old High German *beraht*, meaning "bright," referring to "a good, bright passageway in a mountain range."

Colby From the Old English and Danish, meaning "a coal town."

Cole A pet form of Coleman or Colby.

Coleman, Colman From the Middle English *col*, meaning "coal," hence "coal miner." Or, from the Middle English *cole* and the Latin *colis*, meaning "cabbage," hence "a man who farms cabbage."

Colin Most often, a pet form of Nicholas, meaning "victory."

Collier From the Middle English *col*, meaning "a coal miner." Also, "a ship for carrying coal." Collie is a pet form.

Connor, Conor   An Irish form of Conan, from the Middle English *connen*, meaning "to be able, to be knowledgeable."

Conrad   From the Old High German, meaning "bold, wise counsellor."

Conroy   A variant form of Conrad.

Conway   A Welsh place-name, meaning "head river."

Cooper   From the Latin *cupa*, meaning "a cask." An occupational name for persons who make and repair barrels.

Corbet, Corbett   From the Old French *corb* and the Middle English *corbe*, meaning "a raven, a crow."

Corby   A pet form of Corbet.

Cordell   From the Old French *corde* and the Latin *chorda*, meaning "a rope."

Corey   A variant form of Cory.

Corin   From the Greek *kore*, meaning "a maiden." A masculine form of Cora.

Cornelius   From the Old French *cornille* and *corneille*, derived from the Latin *cornicula*, meaning "a cornell tree."

Cornell   A variant form of Cornelius.

Corwan   A variant spelling of Corwin.

Corwin   From the Latin *corvinus*, meaning "a raven." Akin to Corbet.

Cory   From the Latin *korys,* meaning "a helmet." Corey is a variant spelling. Also, a pet form of Cornelius.

Cosmo   From the Greek *kosmos,* meaning "universe, universal."

Courtenay, Courtney   From the Late Latin *curtis,* meaning "an enclosed place."

Courtland, Courtlandt   From the Anglo-Saxon, meaning "land belonging to the king (court)."

Court, Courts   From the Late Latin *curtis,* meaning "an enclosed area." Akin to Curtis.

Covington   From the Anglo-Saxon *cofa,* meaning "a cove, a cave, a secret place," hence "the town near the cove."

Cowan   From the Middle English *coul* and the Latin *capa,* meaning "a hooded cloak," hence, a member of the clergy. Akin to Cohen, from the Hebrew, meaning "priest."

Craig   From the Celtic and Gaelic *creag,* meaning "from the crag or rugged rocky mass." Graig is a variant form.

Cramer   From the Middle English *crammen,* meaning "to cram in, to squeeze in." Akin to Kramer. Originally an occupational name for a peddler who traveled the country with a cram (pack) on his back.

Crandall, Crandell   From the Old English, meaning "a dale, a valley of cranes."

Crane   From the Old English *cran,* meaning "to cry hoarsely." A member of the family of large wading birds.

Crawford From the Old English, meaning "the ford or stream where the crows flock."

Creston From the Old English, meaning "Christ's town."

Cristobal A compound of the French *bal*, meaning "to dance," and Christ, hence "the dance of Christ."

Cristobol A variant form of Cristobal.

Crockett From the British *crug*, meaning "a heap, a hill."

Crosby From the Anglo-Saxon, meaning "a crossroads near the town." Or, from the Middle English, meaning "the cross in the town."

Crowell From the Middle English *crowe* and the German *krake*, meaning "to crow, to call," hence "a cry of victory."

Cullen From the Celtic, meaning "a cub, a young animal." May also be a corrupt form of Cologne (Koln) in Germany.

Culley A pet form of Cullen.

Culver From the Latin *columba* and the Old English *culfer*, meaning "a dove."

Curt A pet form of Curtis. Kurt is a variant form.

Curtis From the Late Latin *curtis*, meaning "an enclosure, a court." Or, from the Old French *corteis*, meaning "courteous." Akin to Court.

Cy A pet form of Cyrus.

Cyril From the Greek, meaning "lordly."

Cyrus   From the Persian, meaning "sun." In the Bible, a king of Persia (c. 600-529 B.C.).

Dale   From the Old English *dael*, and the Old Norse *dalr*, meaning "a hollow; a small valley."

Dalton   From the Old English, meaning "the town near the valley."

Damien   From the Greek, meaning "divine power" or "fate."

Dan   From the Hebrew, meaning "judge."

Daniel   From the Hebrew, meaning "God is my judge." In the Bible, a character noted for his escape from the lion's den.

Darnell   The name of a weed found in grain fields, resembling rye, and sometimes called rye grass.

Darrel, Darrell   Variant forms of Darlin, from the British *dar*, meaning "a grove of oak trees."

Darren   From the British, meaning "a small, rocky hill."

Darrow   From the Old English *daroth*, meaning "a spear."

Darton   From the British *dwr* plus the Old English *ton*, meaning "the town near the water."

Darwin   From the British and Anglo-Saxon, meaning "lover of the sea."

David   From the Hebrew, meaning "beloved." In the Bible, the second king of Israel, successor to King Saul; father of King Solomon.

Dayman, Daymon, Daymond From the Anglo-Saxon *daeg,* meaning "day." Dag, Damien, and Damon are variant forms.

Dean, Deane From the Old French *deien,* meaning "head, leader." Also, from the Celtic *den* and the Old English *dean* and *dene,* meaning "a hollow, a small valley."

Dee Probably derived from the name of the river.

Delmar From the Latin, meaning "of the sea." Delmer and Delmore are variant spellings. Del is a pet form.

Demetrius From the Greek, meaning "lover of the earth."

Demond A short form of Desmond.

Dempsey From the Middle English and Old French *demerite,* meaning "deserving of blame, demerit."

Denis The French form of the Latin and Greek name Dionysus.

Dennis A variant spelling of Denis.

Denver From the Anglo-Saxon and Old French, meaning "green valley."

Derek An English form of the Old High German name Hrodrich, meaning "famous ruler."

Dermot From the British and Middle English, meaning "a pond surrounding a castle."

Derry From the British *deru,* meaning "oak tree."

Derwin, Derwyn From the British *dwr,* meaning "water," hence "a lover of water, a sailor."

Desi   An abbreviated form of Desiderio, from the Latin, meaning "desire." Also, a pet form of Desmond.

Desmond   From the French and Latin *mundus*, meaning "the world, society." Des, Desi, and Dezi are pet forms.

Dewey   A Welsh form of David.

Dietrich   From the German, meaning "a rich people."

Dillon   A variant form of Dale. Or, a variant spelling of Dylan.

Dimitri   A variant form of Demetrius.

Dion   A short form of Dionysius, the god of wine and revelry in Greek mythology.

Dom   A pet form of Dominic.

Dominic, Dominick   From the Latin *dominicus*, meaning "belonging to, pertaining to God."

Don   A pet form of Donald. Also, the Spanish form of the Latin *dominus*, meaning "master."

Donahue   A variant form of Donald.

Donald   From the Irish form Donghal, meaning "brown stranger." Donal is a popular Irish variant form. Also, from the Celtic and Scottish, meaning "proud ruler." Don, Donnie, and Donny are pet forms.

Donnelly   A variant form of Donnel, from the Celtic *don* and *dun*, meaning "a hill."

Donovan   A variant form of Donald.

Dorian   A variant form of Dore and Doran, from the Greek, meaning "a gift." Also, from the Greek, meaning "from the town of Doris," where one group of ancient Greeks lived.

Doug   A pet form of Douglas.

Douglas   From the Celtic, meaning "gray." Also, from the Gaelic, meaning "black stream."

Dow, Dowe   Variant forms of David.

Drake   From the Latin *draco*, meaning "a dragon." Or, from the Old High German, meaning "a male duck."

Drew   A pet form of Andrew.

Dryden   From the Anglo-Saxon, meaning "a dry valley."

Duane   A variant form of Wayne.

Duke   From the Latin, meaning "leader." The nickname of actor John Wayne.

Duncan   From the Celtic, meaning "a warrior with dark skin." Dunc is a pet form.

Durwald   From the Old English, meaning "a forest of wild animals."

Durwin   From the Old English, meaning "a friend of the animal world." Dirk is a pet form.

Dustin   A variant form of Dunstan, from the Old English, meaning "the brownrock quarry."

Dwayne   A variant form of Wayne.

Dwight   From the Anglo-Saxon, meaning "white, fair."

Dylan   From the Welsh, meaning "the sea."

&

Earl   From the Middle English *erl*, meaning "a nobleman, a count." Or, from the Anglo-Saxon *eorl*, meaning "warrior, brave man."

Eaton   From the Anglo-Saxon, meaning "the town near the river."

Ed   A pet form of Edward.

Edan   From the Celtic, meaning "fire, flame."

Eddie   A pet form of Edward.

Eddy   From the Middle English *ydy*, meaning "a whirlpool." Also, a pet form of Edward.

Edgar   From the Anglo-Saxon name Eadgar, de-rived from *ead*, meaning "riches," plus *gar*, mean-ing "a spear."

Edison   A patronymic form, meaning "the son of Ed (Edward)."

Edmond, Edmund   From the Anglo-Saxon name Eadmund. Derived from *ead*, meaning "rich, fortu-nate, happy," and *mund (mond)*, meaning "warrior, protector."

Edward   From the Old English name Eadweard, derived from *ead*, meaning "happy, fortunate," and *weard*, meaning "guardian, protector," hence "happy guardian."

Edwin   From the Old English name Eadwine. Derived from *ead*, meaning "happy," and *win*, meaning "friend."

Elden   A variant form of Elder. Akin to Eldon. From the Middle English *elde*, meaning "old age, antiquity."

Eldwin   From the Old English, meaning "noble friend" or "old friend."

Eli   From the Hebrew *al*, meaning "on, up, high."

Elijah   From the Hebrew, meaning "the Lord is my God."

Elliot, Elliott   Variant forms of Elijah.

Ellis   A variant form of Elisha, from the Hebrew, meaning "God is my salvation."

Elroy, El Roy   From the Latin, meaning "royal, king." The French form is Leroy.

Elton   From the Anglo-Saxon, meaning "from the old farm or village."

Elva   An Old English variant form of Elvin.

Elvin   From the Anglo-Saxon *aelfwine*, meaning "friend *(wine),*" and "noble (aelf)," hence "noble friend."

Elvis   A variant form of Elvin.

Elwin   A variant form of Elvin.

Ely   A variant spelling of Eli. Or, from the Old English, meaning "island of eels."

Emanuel   From the Hebrew, meaning "God is with us." In the Bible, the name appears in Isaiah 7:14, and is said to refer to the Messiah.

Emil   From the Latin *aemulus*, meaning "to emulate, to be industrious."

Emmanuel   A variant spelling of Emanuel.

Emmitt   A variant spelling of Emmett, from the Hebrew *emet*, meaning "truth." Or, from the Anglo-Saxon, meaning "an ant."

Emmon   A variant spelling of Eamon.

Emory   A variant spelling of Emery, from the Old High German name Amalrich, meaning "work" and "ruler."

Enrico   An Italian form of Henry.

Enzio   An Italian form of Henry. Or, a variant form of Enzo.

Enzo   A variant form of Enzio.

Ephraim   From the Hebrew, meaning "fruitful." In the Bible, one of the two sons of Joseph. Efraim is a variant spelling. Efrem is a variant form.

Ephron   From the Hebrew, meaning "a fawn." In the Bible, a Hittite who sold Abraham a burial plot. Efron is a variant spelling.

Eric   From the Old Norse name Eirkir, a compound of the German *chre*, meaning "honor," and the Latin *rex*, meaning "king, ruler," hence "honorable ruler."

Erich   A variant spelling of Eric.

Erik   A variant spelling of Eric.

Ernest   From the Old High German *ernust*, meaning "resolute, earnest, sincere."

Errol   From the Latin *errare*, meaning "to wander."

Ervin, Erwin   Variant forms of Irvin.

Esteban   The Spanish form of Stephen.

Etan, Ethan   From the Hebrew, meaning "permanent, firm, strong." Etan is the modern Hebrew spelling. In the Bible, a son of Zera; a descendant of Gershon; a Levite.

Eugene   From the Greek, meaning "well born, born lucky" or "one of noble descent."

Evan   A Welsh form of John.

Evans   A patronymic form of Evan, meaning "son of Evan."

Everard, Everhard   From the Norse and German, meaning "a strong, wild boar."

Everett   From the Old High German name Eburhart, derived from *ebur*, meaning "a wild boar," and *harto*, meaning "hard, strong," hence "one who is strong; a warrior."

Everley   From Old English, meaning "Ever's (Everett's) field."

Ewald   A variant form of Evald.

Ezra   From the Hebrew, meaning "help, salvation."

Fabian   From the Latin name Fabianus, meaning "belonging to Fabius."

Fairleigh, Fairley   From the Anglo-Saxon, meaning "the wayside place." Farley is a variant form.

Felipe   The Spanish form of Philip.

Felix   From the Latin *felix*, meaning "happy, fortunate, prosperous." The name of four popes and a number of saints.

Felton   From the Old English, meaning "the town in the garden."

Fenton   From the Old English, meaning "the town near the fen or marsh."

Floyd   A corrupt form of Lloyd.

Forester   An Old French occupational name, meaning "one in charge of a forest."

Forrest   From the Latin *foris*, "out-of-doors, woods."

Foster   A variant form of Forrest.

Fowler   From the Old English *fugol* and the German *vogel*, meaning "one who traps fowl (birds)." Falconer, Falkner, and Faulkner are variant forms.

Francesco, Francisco   Variant forms of Francis.

Francis   From the Middle Latin name Franciscus, meaning "a free man."

Franciscus   The Middle Latin form of Francis.

Frank   A pet form of Francis. From the Old English name Franca and the Old French name Franc, meaning "a Frank," hence "a free man."

Franklin   A Middle English form of the Late Latin name Francus plus the Germanic suffix *ling*, meaning "freeholder." Akin to Francis.

Fred, Freddie, Freddy   Pet forms of Frederick.

Frederic   A variant spelling of Frederick.

Frederick   From the Old High German *fridu*, meaning "peace," plus *rik*, a form of the Latin *rex*, meaning "king, ruler."

Fritz   A German variant form of Frederick.

Fulbert   From the Old German name Filibert, compounded of *filu*, meaning "much," and *berhta*, meaning "bright." Fulbright, and Philbert are variant forms.

Fulbright   A variant English form of Fulbert.

Fuller   From the Old English *fullere*, meaning "a person whose job it is to full (shrink and thicken) cloth." A popular occupational surname.

Fulton   From the Anglo-Saxon, meaning "a field near the town."

Gabe   A pet form of Gabriel.

Gabriel   From the Hebrew, meaning "God is my strength."

Gaines   From the Middle English and French, meaning "to increase in wealth."

Gale   From the German *gagel*, meaning "a hardy shrub."

Galen   From the Greek, meaning "still, tranquil."

Gali   From the Hebrew, meaning "my wave."

Garcia   From the Anglo-Saxon *gar*, meaning "a spear."

Gareth   A variant form of Garth.

Garett   A variant form of Garth.

Garfield   From the Old English *gara*, meaning "a promontory."

Garner   From the Middle English *gerner* and the Latin *granarium*, meaning "a granary."

Garnet, Garnett   From the Latin *granatum*, meaning "a grain, a seed," and literally "a pomegranate," whose seed resembles the precious red jewel named garnet.

Garrard   A variant form of the German name Gerhard, akin to the Old French Gerard.

Garret, Garreth, Garrett   From the Old French *garir*, meaning "to watch." Akin to Garth. Gary is a pet form.

Garrison   From the Old French *garison*, meaning "a garrison, troops stationed at a fort."

Garth   From the Old Norse *gyrthr*, meaning "an enclosure, a field, a garden."

Garvey, Garvie   From the Anglo-Saxon, meaning "a spear-bearer, a warrior." Also, forms of Garth.

Gary, Garry   Variant forms of Garvey.

Gayle   A pet form of Gaylord, from the Old French *gailard,* meaning "brave."

Gene   A pet form of Eugene.

Gennaro   An Italian form of John. Gino is a pet form.

Geno   An Italian and Greek form of John.

Geoffrey   From the Anglo-Saxon, meaning "gift of peace."

George   From the Greek, meaning "a farmer" or "a tiller of the soil."

Gerald   An Old French and Old High German form of Gerard.

Gerard   A variant form of the Old French *gerart.* Akin to the Old High German name Gerhart. From *ger,* meaning "spear," implying "a warrior."

Gerhard, Gerhardt, Gerhart   Variant forms of Gerard.

Gerome   From the Greek, meaning "of holy fame" or "sacred name." Jerome is a variant spelling.

Gerry   A pet form of Gerome.

Gervis   A variant form of Gervais, from the Old German *ger,* meaning "spear."

Gibson A patronymic, meaning "son of Gib (Gilbert)."

Gideon From the Hebrew, meaning either "maimed" or "a mighty warrior."

Gifford A variant form of Gilford.

Gil From the Hebrew, meaning "joy." Used also as a feminine name in Israel. Also, a pet form of Gilbert.

Gilbert From the Old High German name Willibehrt, meaning "to will, to desire," plus "bright" (*behrt*), hence "the will to be bright (famous)."

Giles From the Greek *aegis*, meaning "goatskin," hence "a shield that protects."

Gilford From the Old English, meaning "a ford near the wooded ravine."

Gilles A variant spelling of Giles.

Gillian A variant form of Giles.

Gino The Italian pet form of John. Akin to Gennaro.

Giorgio The Italian form of George.

Girard A variant spelling of Gerard.

Glen, Glenn From the Celtic, meaning "a glen, a dale; a secluded, woody valley."

Godfrey From the Old German name Godafrid, meaning "God's peace."

Godwin From the Anglo-Saxon, meaning "friend of God."

Gomer From the Hebrew, meaning "to end, to complete."

Goodwin From the Anglo-Saxon, meaning "good, faithful friend." Godwin is a variant form.

Gordon From the Old English *gor* and *denn*, meaning "a dung pasture." May also be a form of Gordius, meaning "bold."

Gore A short form of Gordon.

Grady From the Latin *gradus*, meaning "a grade, a rank."

Graham From the Anglo-Saxon, meaning "the gray home."

Granger From the Old French, meaning "a farm steward."

Grant From the Middle English and Old French, meaning "to give, to assure."

Granville, Grenville From the French, meaning "the big town."

Gray From the Old English *graeg*, meaning "to shine." Also a color.

Grayson From the Anglo-Saxon, meaning "the son of a *greve* (an earl)." Or, a patronymic form of Gray.

Greg From the Anglo-Saxon *graeg*, meaning "to shine." Also a pet form of Gregory.

Gregor The German and Scandinavian form of Gregory.

Gregory From the Greek, meaning "vigilant," hence "watchman."

Griffin   A mythological animal with the body and hind legs of a lion, and the head and wings of an eagle.

Griffith   From the Welsh name Gruffydd, a variant form of Griffin.

Grover   From the Anglo-Saxon, meaning "one who grows or tends to trees."

Gunther   From the Old German *gundi*, meaning "war."

Gus   A pet form of Gustave.

Gustav   The German form of Gustavus.

Gustave   The French form of Gustavus.

Gustavo   The Italian and Spanish form of Gustavus.

Gustavus   From the German and Swedish, meaning "the staff of the Goths."

Guthrie   From the Celtic, meaning "war serpent" or "war hero."

Guy   From the Old French, meaning "a guide" or "a rope that guides." Also, from the Hebrew, meaning "valley."

H

Hadley   From the Old English, meaning "the meadow near the wasteland (heath)."

Hal   A pet form of Harold or Haley.

Haldon   From the Old English, meaning "Hal's (Harold's) town."

Hale From the Old English *hal,* meaning "healthy, whole."

Haley, Halley Variant forms of Hale.

Halford From the Old English, meaning "Hal's (Harold's) ford (river crossing)."

Halil, Hallil From the Hebrew, meaning "a flute."

Hammond From the Old English, meaning "a home" or "a village."

Hamon From the Old German name Haimo, derived from *haimi,* meaning "home, house."

Hampton From the Old English, meaning "a town" or "a village."

Hans, Hanns A short form of the German name Johannes. Dutch, German, and Swedish forms of John.

Hanson A patronymic form, meaning "the son of Hans (John)."

Harald A Norse form of Harold, from the Old Norse name Harivald.

Hardin A variant form of Hardy.

Harding A variant form of Hardy.

Hardy From the Middle English and Old French, meaning "bold, robust."

Harlan From the Middle English *herle,* and the Low German *harle,* meaning "a strand of hemp or flax."

Harley   From the Old English, meaning "a field in which plants yielding hemplike fiber grow." Akin to Harlan.

Harman   A form of the Anglo-Saxon name Herenan, meaning "army man, soldier." Akin to Herman.

Harmon   From the Greek, meaning "peace, harmony." Or, a variant spelling of Harman.

Harold   From the Old English name Hereweald and the Germanic name Hariwald, meaning "leader of the army." Akin to Herbert. Hal is a common pet form.

Harper   From the Old Norse *harpa*, meaning "to grip a javelin for spearing whales."

Harrison   A patronymic form, meaning "Harry's son."

Harry   From the Middle English name Herry, a form of Henry.

Hart, Harte   From the Middle English *hert*, akin to the German name Hirsch, meaning "a hart, a deer, a stag."

Hartley   From the Old English, meaning "a field in which the deer roam."

Hartman   A variant form of Hart, meaning "a man who traps or deals with deers."

Harvey   From the Old High German *herewig*, meaning "army battle." Harve is short form. Herve is a French variant.

Hasting, Hastings   From the Latin *hasta*, meaning "a spear."

Hayward From the Middle English *hei*, meaning "a hedge," and *ward*, meaning "a guardian," hence "a protective fence or hedge."

Haywood, Heywood From the Old English, meaning "a hay field." Akin to Hayward.

Heath From the Middle English, meaning "wasteland."

Hector From the Greek, meaning "anchor." In Greek mythology, Hector was the son of Priam. He was slain by Achilles.

Henderson A variant form of Anderson, a patronymic of Andrew.

Henri The French form of Henry.

Henry From the Old High German names Haimirich and Heimerich, compounded of *haimi*, meaning "house, home," and *ric*, meaning "ruler."

Herbert From the Old English *herebeorht*, meaning "bright, excellent army or ruler."

Herman From the Old High German name Hariman, meaning "army *(heri)* man" or "soldier." Akin to Harold.

Hermann A variant German form of Herman.

Heron A variant form of Hern. Heron of Alexandria, a third-century A.D. Greek mathematician and inventor.

Hersch, Hersh From the German, meaning "a deer." Hertz, Hertzl, Heschel, and Heshel, are variant forms. Hirsch and Hirsh are variant spellings.

Herschel, Hershel   A diminutive form of Hersch.

Herzl   A diminutive form of Hirsch. From the German, meaning "a deer."

Heschel, Heshel   Variant forms of Hersch and Herschel.

Hew   A pet form of Hewlett or a variant spelling of Hugh.

Hewlett   From the British *aewelm*, meaning "the fountainhead of a stream." The "h" is aspirated.

Heywood   From the Old English, meaning "a field on which hay is grown."

Hilary   From the Greek and Latin, meaning "cheerful."

Hillel   From the Hebrew, meaning "praised, famous." In the Bible, the father of a Hebrew judge.

Hilliard   A variant form of Hillard and Hilary.

Hiraldo   A Spanish form of Harold.

Hiram   From the Hebrew, meaning "noble born" or "exalted brother."

Hodding   From the Middle Dutch *hodde*, meaning "a wooden tray for carrying bricks," hence "bricklayer." Or, from the Anglo-Saxon, meaning "a heath near water."

Hodge, Hodges   Variant forms of Roger and Rogers, from the Old High German name Hrodger, meaning "famous spear."

Hogan   An Irish variant form of Hagan and Haven. Also, from the language of the Navajo Indians, meaning "house."

Holden   From the Old English, meaning "a valley."

Holt   From the Old English and the German *holz*, meaning "wood," hence "a wooded area."

Horace   From the Greek, meaning "to see, to behold." The Latin form is Horatius.

Horatio   The Italian form of Horace.

Horatius   The Latin form of Horace.

Horst   From the German, meaning "a thicket."

Horton   From the Latin *hortus*, meaning "a garden."

Howard   From the Anglo-Saxon, meaning "guardian of the home."

Hubert   From the Old High German name Huguberht, meaning "bright in mind and spirit *(hugu)*."

Hudson   A patronymic form, meaning "son of Hudd."

Huey   A pet form of Hubert.

Hugh   A pet form of Hubert.

Hugo   A variant form of Hugh.

Humberto   The Spanish form of the Italian Umberto.

Humphrey, Humphry   From the Old English *hunfrith*, derived from the Germanic *hun*, meaning "strength," and the Old English *frith*, meaning "peace."

Hunt, Hunter, Huntington   From the Old English *huntian*, meaning "to search, hunt."

Hutchins   Originally a surname derived from Hodges, a form of Roger.

Huxley   From the Anglo-Saxon, meaning "a field of ash trees."

Hyde   From the Old English *hida*, meaning "a measure of land."

Hyland   From the Anglo-Saxon, meaning "one who lives on high land."

I

Ian   The Scottish form of John.

Ignatius   From the Greek and Latin, meaning "the fiery or lively one."

Igor   From the Scandinavian, meaning "hero."

Ike   A pet form of Isaac.

Immanuel   From the Hebrew, meaning "God is with us."

Ingmar   From the Old English *ing*, meaning "meadow," and *mare*, meaning "sea."

Ingram   From the British *engylion*, meaning "angel."

Inness, Innis   From the British, meaning "an island."

Ira   From the Hebrew *yarod*, meaning "descend." Akin to Jordan.

Irvin, Irvine, Irving From the Gaelic, meaning "beautiful, handsome, fair."

Irwin, Irwyn A variant spelling of Irvin.

Isaac From the Hebrew *yitzchak*, meaning "he will laugh."

Isador, Isadore Variant spellings of Isidor, from the Greek, meaning "gift of Isis."

Israel From the Hebrew, meaning either "prince of God" or "wrestled with God."

Itamar From the Hebrew, meaning "island of palms."

Ivan The Russian form of John, meaning "grace."

J

Jack A pet form of Jacob.

Jacob From the Hebrew, meaning "held by the heel," hence "one who holds back another."

Jacobo A Spanish form of Jacob.

Jacque, Jacques French forms of Jacob.

Jaeson A variant spelling of Jason.

Jaime A Spanish pet form of James.

Jake A pet form of Jacob.

Jakob A variant spelling of Jacob.

James The English form of the Hebrew name Jacob, meaning "held by the heel, supplanter."

Jamie   A Scottish pet form of James.

Jan   A form of either John or James. Sometimes used as an independent name.

Jared   From the Hebrew, meaning "to descend" or "descendant." In the Bible, an ancestor of Noah. Jordan is a related name.

Jarib   From the Hebrew, meaning "he will contend."

Jaron   From the Hebrew, meaning "to sing, cry out."

Jarrell   A variant form of Gerald.

Jarrett   A variant form of Garret.

Jarrod   A variant form of Jared.

Jarvis   From the Old English name Garwig, meaning "a battle spear," hence "a conqueror."

Jason   From the Greek and Latin, meaning "healer."

Jaspar, Jasper   From the Greek, meaning "a semi-precious stone."

Jay   From the Old French and Latin *gaius*, referring to a bird in the crow family.

Jean   The French form of John.

Jed   From the Arabic, meaning "hand."

Jef, Jeff   Short forms of Jeffery and Geoffrey.

Jefferson   A patronymic form, meaning "the son of Jeffers or Jeffery."

Jeffery, Jefferey From the Anglo-Saxon, meaning "gift of peace" or "God's peace." Variant forms of Geoffrey. Jef and Jeff are pet forms.

Jenner A variant form of John.

Jerald A variant spelling of Gerald.

Jeremy A pet form of Jeremiah.

Jerold, Jerrold Variant spellings of Gerald.

Jerome From the Greek, meaning "of holy name." A fourth-century monk who translated the Bible into Latin.

Jerrald A variant spelling of Jerold.

Jerrel A variant form of Jarrell and Gerald.

Jesse From the Hebrew *yishai*, meaning "wealthy" or "a gift."

Jethro From the Hebrew, meaning "abundance, riches." In the Bible, the father-in-law of Moses.

Jim A pet form of James, evolved by shortening the long "a" sound.

Jimmie, Jimmy Popular pet forms of James.

Joab From the Hebrew, meaning "willing" or "God is father."

Job From the Hebrew, meaning "hated, oppressed."

Jody A pet form of Joseph.

Joe, Joey Pet forms of Joseph.

Joel From the Hebrew, meaning "God is willing." In the Bible, one of the twelve minor prophets.

Johanan A variant spelling of Jochanan, from the Hebrew, meaning "God is gracious, merciful."

Johannes A Middle Latin form of John.

John From the Hebrew, meaning "God is gracious; God is merciful."

Jon A pet form of Jonathan.

Jonathan From the Hebrew, meaning "God has given." In the Bible, the son of King Saul; friend and brother-in-law of David.

Jordan From the Hebrew *yarod*, meaning "to flow down, descend," hence "a descendant."

Jorel A name invented by combining *Joyce* and *Reuel*.

Jorge A Spanish form of George.

Jori, Jory Pet forms of Jordan.

Jose A Spanish form of Joseph.

Joseph From the Hebrew name Yosayf, meaning "He (God) will add or increase."

Josephus The Latin form of Joseph.

Josh A pet form of Joshua and Josiah.

Joshua From the Hebrew, meaning "the Lord is my salvation."

Josiah From the Hebrew, meaning "fire of the Lord."

Jotham From the Hebrew, meaning "God is perfect." In the Bible, the youngest of Gideon's seventy sons. Also, a king of Judah.

Jud A variant spelling of Judd, derived from Judah or Jordan.

Judd A variant form of Judah or Jordan.

Judson A patronymic form of Judah, meaning "Judah's (or Judd's) son."

Jule, Jules Variant forms of Julian or Julius.

Julian Origin uncertain, but probably from the Greek, meaning "soft-haired, light-bearded."

Julio The Spanish form of Julian and Julius.

Julius A variant form of Julian.

Jurgen A Germanic form of George.

Justin A variant form of Justus.

Justino An Italian form of Justus.

Justus From the Latin, meaning "just." Justus is the Latin form.

𝒦

Kahil From the Arabic, meaning "friend, lover."

Kal Possibly a short form of Kalil.

Kalil From the Greek *kalos*, meaning "beautiful."

Kane A variant form of Keene.

Kaniel From the Hebrew, meaning "a reed, a stalk," or from the Arabic, meaning "a spear."

Kareem From the Arabic, meaning "noble, exalted." Karim is a variant spelling.

Karel A variant form of Carol and Charles.

Karim A variant spelling of Kareem.

Karl A variant spelling for Carl, a form of Charles.

Karol, Karole Variant spellings of Carol.

Kay Either from the Greek, meaning "rejoicing," or from a Germanic root, meaning "a fortified place" or "a warden."

Kaz A pet form of Cassius, from the Old Norman French *casse* meaning "a protective cover."

Kean, Keane Variant forms of Keene.

Kearney, Kearny Variant forms of Kern.

Keenan A variant form of Keene.

Keene From the Old English *cene*, meaning "wise, learned," and the German *kuhn*, meaning "bold."

Keir A variant form of Kerr.

Keith From the Gaelic, meaning "the wind." A popular name in Scotland.

Kelly From the Old English *ceol*, meaning "a keel, a ship," and the Dutch and the Old Norse *kill*, meaning "a stream, river, inlet," hence "the ship on or near the river."

Kelson   From the Middle Dutch *kiel,* meaning "a boat."

Kelton   From the Old English, meaning "keel town," or "the town where ships are built." Akin to Kelson.

Kelvin, Kelwin   From the Anglo-Saxon, meaning "a friend or lover of ships."

Ken   A short form of Kenneth.

Kendal, Kendall   From the Celtic, meaning "ruler of the valley."

Kendrick   From the Anglo-Saxon *coenric,* meaning "royal."

Kene   A variant spelling of Kenny, the pet form of Kenneth.

Kenley   From the British, meaning "headland, peninsula."

Kenman   From Old English, meaning "leadman, ruler."

Kenn   A pet form of Kenneth.

Kenneth   From the Scottish and Gaelic *caioreach,* meaning "comely, handsome."

Kent   A variant form of Kenneth.

Kenton   A variant form of Kent and Kenneth.

Kermit   A variant form of the Dutch *kermis,* meaning "a church."

Kern   From the Old Irish *ceitern,* meaning "a band of soldiers."

Kerr From the Norse, meaning "marshland." Carr is a variant form.

Kerry A variant form of Kerr.

Kerwin From the Old English, meaning "a friend of the marshlands."

Ketti A variant form of the Old English surnames Kettle and Kittle, meaning "cauldron (of the gods)."

Kevin From the Gaelic, meaning "handsome, beautiful." Coemgen is the Old Irish form.

Kile A variant spelling of Kyle.

Kilian From the British *kil*, meaning "a cell, a retreat."

Kilmer From the Dutch and French, meaning "an inlet to the sea" or "a retreat near the sea."

Kim A pet form of Kimball or Kimberly. Used also as a feminine name.

Kirby From the Old English *ciric* and *cirice* and the Middle English *kirke*, meaning "a church." Or, from the British, meaning "a cottage by the water."

Kirk The Scottish form of the Middle English *kirke* and the Old English *ciric* and *cirice*, meaning "a church."

Kirkland From the Old English, meaning "church's land." Kirtland is a variant form.

Kit A pet form of Christopher.

Kitron From the Hebrew, meaning "crown."

Kivi A short form of Akiba, Yaakov, or Jacob.

Knox   From the British *knock (cnwee),* meaning "a bunch or swelling," hence "a hill."

Kraig   A variant spelling of Craig.

Kramer   A variant spelling of Cramer.

Kresten   A Danish form of Christian.

Kris, Kristian   Variant forms of Christian and Christopher.

Kurt   A pet form of Konrad, variant of Conrad.

Kyle   A Gaelic form of the Old English name Kyloe, meaning "a hill where the cattle graze." Kile is a variant spelling.

L

Laban   From the Hebrew, meaning "white."

Labron   From the French *brun,* meaning "brown." A variant form of Bruno.

Ladd, Laddie   From the Middle English *ladde,* meaning "a boy."

Lafayette   From the Old French *fei,* meaning "faith."

Laird   A form of Lord, which in Scotland refers to wealthy landowners.

Lale, Lalo   From the Latin *lallare,* meaning "to sing a lullaby."

Lamar, LaMar   From the Latin and French, meaning "of the sea."

Lambert   From the German and French, meaning "the brightness of the land." Lamberto is the Italian form.

Lammie   A pet form of either Lambert or Lamar.

LaMont, Lamont   From the Latin, French, and Spanish, meaning "the mountain."

Lance   From the Latin *lancea,* meaning "a light spear." Lancelot is a pet form.

Lander, Landers   Possibly a short form of Flanders, once an independent country to the north of France.

Landis   A variant form of Landan, from the Anglo-Saxon *launde,* meaning "an open, grassy area; a lawn."

Landon   A variant form of Landan.

Landry   A variant form of Landan. From the Old English, meaning "rough (*rih*) land." Langtry is a variant form.

Lane   From the Old English *lanu,* meaning "to move, to go," hence "a narrow path between hedges; a road."

Langdon   A compounded Old English form, meaning "long valley."

Langford   An Old English compounded form, meaning "the long river crossing."

Langley   A variant Old English form of the German *lang,* meaning "the long meadow."

Langston   A compounded Old English name from *lang* and *ton,* meaning "a long narrow town."

Lansing   An Old English patronymic form, meaning "son of Lance."

Larns   A pet form of Laurence.

Larry   A popular pet form of Laurence.

Lars   A Swedish pet form of Laurence.

Larson   A patronymic form of Larns or Lars. Used in Ireland.

Laszlo   Probably a Slovakian form of Lazarus.

Latham   From the Old English *leth* and *lathe*, meaning "a division, a district."

Latimer   From the Old English, meaning "a district near the sea."

Laurence   From the Latin, meaning "a laurel, a crown."

Laval   A French form of Lave.

Lave   From the Old English *hlaford*, meaning "Lord." Also, from the Italian *lave* and the Latin *labes*, meaning "lava, a mountain of molten rock." Akin to Lawton.

Lawrence   A variant spelling of Laurence.

Lawton   From the Old English, meaning "a town on the hill *(hlaew)*."

Lazar   A pet form of Elazar and Lazarus.

Lazarus   The Greek form of the Hebrew name Elazar, meaning "God has helped." In the Bible, the brother of Mary and Martha, raised from the dead by Jesus.

Lazer A Yiddish form of Eliezer, from the Hebrew, meaning "on, up, high."

Lee A pet form of Leo, Leon, Leroy, Leslie, Leigh. Also, a name derived from the Anglo-Saxon, meaning "field, meadow."

Leeland From the Old English *hleo* and the German *lee*, meaning "a shelter, a protected area."

Lee Roy A variant spelling of Leroy.

Leif From the Old Norse *heifr*, meaning "beloved."

Leighland A variant form of Leeland.

Leighton From the Hebrew, meaning "belonging to God."

Leland A variant spelling of Leeland.

Len A pet form of Leonard. Also, from the Old English *len* and *leen*, meaning "a tenant house on a farm."

Lendal From the Old English, meaning "a river near the alder tree."

Lendon From the Old English, meaning "a river near the tenant farmer's house."

Leni A variant spelling of Lennie, a pet form of Leonard.

Lenis From the Latin, meaning "gentle, mild."

Lenn A variant spelling of Len.

Lennart A variant form of Len.

Lennie A pet form of Leonard.

Lennon   From the Old English, meaning "the river near the tenant farmer's house."

Lennox   From the Old English, meaning "the tenant farmer's ox."

Lenwood   From the Old English, meaning "a tenant house in the woods."

Leo   From the Latin, meaning "lion."

Leon   The Greek form of Leo.

Leonard   The Old French form of the Old High German name Lewenhart, meaning "strong as a lion."

Leonardo   An Italian variant form of Leonard.

Leonid   A Russian form of Leo.

Leor   From the Hebrew, meaning "I have light" or "light is mine."

Leroy   An Old French name of Latin origin, meaning "the king" or "royalty." Lee Roy is a variant spelling.

Les   A pet form of Lester and Leslie.

Leshem   From the Hebrew, meaning "a precious stone."

Lesley, Leslie   From the Anglo-Saxon, meaning "a small meadow, a dell." Lee is a popular pet form.

Lester   Originally Leicester, a place-name in England. From the Latin and the Old English *caestre*, meaning "a camp, a protected area." Chester is a variant form.

Lev   From the Hebrew *layv*, meaning "a heart." Also, a Yiddish form of the German Loeb, meaning "a lion." Also a pet form of Levi.

Levant   A Spanish and French form of the Latin *levare*, meaning "to rise." Applies to Eastern countries from the "rising of the sun."

Levi   From the Hebrew, meaning "joined to" or "attendant upon." In the Bible, the third of Jacob's sons. His mother was Leah. Descendants of Levi were the Priests and Levites who served in the Temple in Jerusalem.

Lew   A pet form of Lewis.

Lewes   A variant spelling of Lewis.

Lewi   The Hawaiian form of Levi.

Lewis   An English form of the French name Louis. Also, a variant form of the Welsh name Llewellyn.

Lex   From the Greek, meaning "a word, vocabulary." Lexington is a variant form.

Leyland   A variant spelling of Leeland.

Liddon   From the Old English *hlidan*, meaning "to hide."

Lieber   A Yiddish form from the German *lieb*, meaning "love."

Lin   A variant spelling of Lyn.

Lincoln   From the Old English *lind* and the German *linde*, meaning "lithe, bending, flexible," and referring to the trees of the linden family. Or, from the Old English and Latin, meaning "the camp near the stream." Akin to Lindsey.

Lind, Linde   From the Old English *lind*, and the German *linde*, meaning "lithe, supple, flexible," and referring to the trees of the linden and lime families.

Lindel, Lindell   Variant forms of Lind.

Linden   A variant form of Lind.

Lindley   From the Old English, meaning "the meadow near the linden trees."

Lindon   A variant form of Lind.

Lindsay   A variant form of Lindsey.

Lindsey   From the Old English, meaning "the linden trees near the water."

Lindsy, Linsey   Variant spellings of Lindsey.

Linley   From the Old English, meaning "the meadow near the brook." Akin to Lin.

Linn, Linnie   Variant forms of Lin.

Linton   A variant form of Lind, meaning "the town with the linden trees."

Linwood   A variant spelling of Lynwood.

Lionel, Lionello   Variant forms of Leon.

Liron   From the Hebrew *li* and *ron*, meaning "song is mine."

Litton   From the Old English, meaning "little town."

Livingston   An Anglicized form of the Anglo-Saxon, meaning "Lever's town, Leif's town."

Lloyd   From the Welsh, meaning "grey." Floyd is a variant form.

Logan   From the Middle English *logge* and the Old Norse *lag*, meaning "a felled tree."

Lon   A pet form of Alphonso.

London   From the British, meaning "a fortress of the moon." Probably a site established by the Romans where a temple was erected to worship Diana, the moon goddess.

Lonnie, Lonny   Pet forms of Alphonso.

Lonzo   A variant form of Alphonso.

Loren, Lorence   Variant forms of Laurence.

Lorentz   A variant form of Laurence.

Lorenzo   An Italian form of Laurence.

Lorimer   From the Latin, meaning "a harness maker."

Lorin   A variant spelling of Loren.

Loring   A variant form of Laurence

Lorn, Lorne   Variant forms of Laurence.

Lorry   A variant form of Laurie, a form of Laurence.

Louis   From the Old French name Loeis, and the Old High German name Hluodowig, meaning "famous in battle."

Lovell   A variant form of Lowell.

Lowe   A variant form of the German name Loeb.

Lowell From the Old English, meaning "beloved." Or, from the Old English *low,* meaning "a hill."

Loy A pet form of Loyal.

Lu A pet form of Lucas or Lucius.

Lucas A variant form of Lucius.

Luce From the Old French *lus,* and the Latin *lucius,* a variety of fish similar to pike.

Lucian, Lucien Variant forms of Lucius.

Luciano An Italian form of Lucius.

Lucio An Italian form of Lucius.

Lucius From the Latin *lucere* meaning "light."

Ludlow An English variant form of Ludwig from the Old German name Hluodowig, meaning "famous war."

Luis A Spanish form of Louis.

Luke The English form of Lucius.

Luther From the German, meaning "renowned soldier; famous fighter."

Lyall A variant form of Lyle.

Lyde, Lydell From the Old English *hlith,* meaning "hill," and the Middle English *lyth,* meaning "slope," referring to "hilly pastureland."

Lyell A variant form of Lyle.

Lyle A variant form of Lisle. From the Spanish, meaning "strong cotton thread."

Lyme   From the Old English *lim*, meaning "lime or mud."

Lyn   From the Old English *hlynna*, meaning "a brook."

Lyndall   A variant form of Lind.

Lynden   A variant spelling of Lyndon.

Lyndon   A variant form of Lind.

Lynley   From the Old English, meaning "the meadow (lea) near the brook."

Lynn   A variant spelling of Lyn.

Lyons   The English form of Lyon (French).

𝓜

Mac   An Irish and Gaelic patronymic form prefixed to many personal names, meaning "son of." Used also as an independent name.

Macey   A variant form of Mace, an English form of the Old French *masse*, meaning "a club," hence a symbol of authority.

Mack   A variant form of Mac.

Maclean   A patronymic form, meaning "the son of Leander."

Macy   A variant spelling of Macey.

Madison   A patronymic form of Maude, meaning "son of Maude." Also, from the British *mad* and *made*, meaning "good."

Malcolm From the Arabic, meaning "a dove." Or, from the Celtic name Maolcolm, meaning "servant of St. Columba." Mal is a common pet form of Malcolm.

Manchester From the Old English, meaning "a fortification, army camp."

Mandel From the Old French *amande*, and the Middle Latin *amandola*, meaning "an almond." Mandy is a pet form.

Manford From the Anglo-Saxon, meaning "a small crossing over a brook."

Manfred From the German name Manifred, meaning "man of peace."

Mani A pet form of Manuel.

Manning From the Old English, meaning "to man, to garrison, to protect."

Manny A pet form of Emanuel or Manfred.

Manuel A short form of Emanuel.

Marc The French form of Marcus.

Marcel A French pet form of Marc and Marcus.

Marcello An Italian form of the French Marcel.

Marcus From the Latin name Mars, meaning "warlike." In Roman mythology, the god of war.

Marcy A variant form of Marcus. Or, from the Old English *mar*, meaning "a pool, a lake."

Marin, Marina, Marino From the Latin *marinus*, meaning "a small harbor."

Mario, Marion   Variant forms of Marian or Marcus.

Maris   From the Old English and French *mare*, meaning "sea, lake."

Marius   A variant form of Marc and Marcus.

Mark   A variant spelling of Marc.

Marlin   From the Latin, Old English, and French *mare*, meaning "sea." A species of deep-sea fish.

Marlo   A variant form of Marlin.

Marlon   A variant spelling of Marlin.

Marques   From the French *marquer*, meaning "a sign, a mark." Also, a variant form of Mark.

Marshal, Marshall   From the Old English *mearh*, meaning "a horse," hence one who grooms a horse; later, one who masters a horse; and, finally, an officer in charge of military matters.

Martin   A French form of the Latin name Martinus. Akin to Marcus, meaning "warlike."

Marvin   From the Old English *mar* plus *win* (vin), meaning "friend of the sea" or "friendly sea."

Mason   From the Old French *macon*, meaning "a mason, a worker in stone."

Massey   A pet form of Massing, from the Old English, meaning "a home where the children of soldiers were housed."

Mathias   A variant form of Mattathias, the Greek form of the Hebrew name Matisyahu, meaning "gift of God."

Matt   A pet form of Matthew.

Matthew   From the Hebrew name Matisyahu, meaning "gift of God."

Maurice   From the Greek *mauros*, the Latin *maurius* and *maurus*, and the Middle English *morys*, meaning "a Moor," and generally associated with a dark-skinned person.

Max, Maxim, Maxime   Short forms of Maximilian, from the Latin *maximus*, meaning "great."

Maxwell   A variant form of Maximilian.

McKinley   A Scottish surname meaning "the son of Kinlay," a name meaning "fair herd."

Melvin   From the Anglo-Saxon *mael*, meaning "council," plus *wine* (vin), meaning "friend." Or, from *mill* plus *win*, meaning "friend of the mill" or "mill worker." Melvyn is a variant spelling.

Merle   From the Latin and French, meaning "blackbird." Used also as a feminine name.

Merlin   A variant form of Merlo, from the French and Italian, meaning "a parapet."

Merrill   A compounded name, from the Old English *mer* and *mere*, meaning "a sea, a pool," and the British and Old English *il* and *iley*, meaning "a river, a body of water."

Mervin, Mervyn   Welsh forms of Marvin.

Meyer   A variant spelling of Mayer, from the Latin *major*, meaning "great."

Michael   From the Hebrew, meaning "Who is like God?" In the Bible, the archangel closest to God;

i.e., the divine messenger who carries out God's judgments.

Mickey   A pet form of Michael.

Miguel   The Spanish and Portuguese forms of Michael.

Mikhail   A Russian form of Michael.

Miles   From the Latin *militatus*, meaning "a warrior, a soldier." Akin to Milan. In England, used as a short form of Michael. Myles is a variant spelling.

Milford   From the Latin *militatus*, meaning "a warrior, a soldier."

Miller   An Old English occupational name, meaning "one who grinds or mills grain."

Milo   A variant form of Miles.

Milton   From the Old English, meaning "the town near the mill."

Mitchel, Mitchell   Variant forms of Michael.

Monroe   An occupational name, from the Scottish *mon*, meaning "man," plus the French *rouer*, from the Latin *rota*, meaning "wheel," hence "a wheeler, one who rolls objects on a wheel."

Montgomery   The English form of Montague, meaning "a hill, a mountain."

Morey   A pet form of Maurice.

Morgan   From the Celtic, meaning "one who lives near the sea."

Morris   A variant form of Maurice.

Morrison   A patronymic form, meaning "the son of Morris."

Morton   From the Old English, meaning "the town near the sea."

Moses   From the Hebrew *mosheh*, meaning "drawn out of (the water)" or from the Egyptian *mes, mesu,* meaning "a son, a child."

Moshe   The exact Hebrew form of Moses.

Murray   From the Celtic *muir*, and the Welsh *mor*, meaning "the sea." Akin to Maurice.

Myer   Variant spellings of Mayer.

Myles   A variant spelling of Miles. *See* Miles.

Myron   From the Greek, meaning "fragrant, sweet, perfumed."

N

Nash, Nashe   From the Old English, meaning "a protruding cliff."

Nathan   From the Hebrew, meaning "He gave," and implying a gift of God.

Nathaniel   From the Hebrew, meaning "gift of God."

Neal, Neale   From the Middle English names Nel, Neel, Nele, and the Gaelic name Niall, meaning "a champion."

Ned   A pet form of Edward.

Neil   A variant spelling of Neal.

Nelson A patronymic form of Neal, meaning "the son of Neal."

Neven, Nevin, Nevins From the Old English *nafa* or *navu*, meaning "the middle," hence "the hub of a wheel."

Nevill, Neville Variant forms of Nevil, from the French, meaning "new village."

Newton From the Anglo-Saxon, meaning "the new town." Originally an English place-name and surname.

Nicholas From the Greek *nike*, meaning "victory," and *laos*, meaning "the people," hence "victory of the people."

Nicolas A variant spelling of Nicholas.

Niel A variant Norse form of Nicholas.

Nigel Probably from the Anglo-Saxon *nyht*, akin to the German *nacht*, meaning "night, dark." Also, possibly a short form of nightingale, meaning "to sing at night."

Nikolai The Russian form of Nicholas.

Niles A patronymic form of Neal, meaning "son of Neal."

Noah From the Hebrew, meaning "rest, peace." In the Bible, the leading character in the story of the flood.

Noble From the Latin *nobilis*, meaning "well known, famous."

Noel From the Old French name Nouel, derived from the Latin *natalis*, meaning "natal; to be born."

Nolan, Noland Probably variant forms of the Anglo-Saxon Northland. Popular in Ireland. May also be from the Celtic, meaning "noble, famous."

Norbert From the German, meaning "divine brightness."

Norman, Normann From the Anglo-Saxon, meaning "a man from the North." Refers to any of the Northmen who conquered Normandy in the tenth century. Normand is a variant form.

Normand A French form of Norman.

Norris From the Anglo-Saxon, meaning "Norman's house" or "a house of a man from the North."

Norwood From the Old English, meaning "the woods in the North."

Nowell A variant form of Noel or Newell.

Nyle A variant Irish form of Neal.

Oliver From the Latin and French, meaning "an olive tree," having the connotation of "peace." May also be from the Germanic *alf*, meaning elf, plus *hari*, meaning "a host, an army." Ollie is a pet form.

Omar From the Arabic, meaning "long life." Omri is a variant form.

Oren From the Hebrew, meaning "a tree (cedar or fir)." In the Bible, a descendant of Judah.

Orien A French form of the Latin name Oriens, meaning "the Orient, the East (where the sun rises)." Akin to Orestes.

Orin, Orrin Variant forms of Orien.

Orland, Orlando A variant form of Roland by metathesis.

Orley A pet form of Orleans, from the Latin *aurum*, meaning "golden."

Orlin A variant form of Orleans.

Orman, Ormand From the Norse *ormr* and *orm*, meaning "a serpent, a worm."

Orrin A variant spelling of Orin.

Orson From the Latin *ursus*, meaning "a bear."

Orville From the French, meaning "golden city." Orval is a variant form.

Osborn, Osborne From the Anglo-Saxon, meaning "divinely strong."

Oscar From the Anglo-Saxon *os*, "a god," plus *gar*, "a spear," hence "divine strength."

Osman, Osmand From the Anglo-Saxon, meaning "servant of God."

Osmond From the Anglo-Saxon, meaning "protected by God."

Ossie A pet form of Oswald or Oscar.

Oswald From the Old English *os*, meaning "a god," and *weald*, meaning "forest," hence "god of the forest."

Otis From the Old Greek, meaning "one who hears well."

Otto High German *otho* and *odo*, meaning "prosperous, wealthy."

Owen Probably a variant Welsh form of the Latin name Eugenius, meaning "well born."

Ozzie A pet form of Oswald.

Paine A variant form of Pagan, from the Latin *paganus*, meaning "a heathen."

Palmer From the Middle English *palmere*, meaning "a pilgrim who carried a palm leaf," as a sign that he had been to the Holy Land.

Park, Parke From the Middle English *parc*, meaning "an enclosed parcel of land."

Pat A pet form of Patrick.

Patrick From the Latin, meaning "a patrician, a person of noble descent."

Paul From the Latin *paulus* or the Greek *paulos*, meaning "small." In the Bible, Paul of Tarsus, an apostle of Christianity. His original name was Saul.

Paxton From the Latin *pax*, meaning "peace," hence "town of peace."

Payton The Scottish form of Patrick.

Pedro A Spanish and Portuguese form of Peter.

Pepe Probably a variant form of Pip, a pet form of Philip.

Perceval, Percival   From the French *perce-val,* meaning "valley piercer." Percival is a later spelling. Percy is a pet form.

Perry   A pet form of Peter.

Peter   From the Greek *petra* and *petros* and the Latin *petrus,* meaning "a rock."

Peyton   A variant spelling of Payton.

Philip, Phillip   From the Greek *philos,* meaning "loving," plus *hippos,* meaning "a horse," hence "a lover of horses."

Pierce   A variant form of Peter.

Pierre   A French form of Peter.

Porter   From the Latin *portare,* meaning "to carry."

Powell   A patronymic Welsh form from ap-Howell, meaning "son of Howell."

Prescott   From the Anglo-Saxon, meaning "the priest's house."

Preston   From the Old English, meaning "priest's town."

Price   From the Middle English and Old French *pris,* meaning "price, value."

Prince   From the Latin *primus,* meaning "first, chief." Akin to Prior.

Pryor   A variant spelling of Prior, from the Latin *primus,* meaning "first, a superior."

Purvis   From the Anglo-French *purveir,* meaning "to provide food."

Q

Quentin, Quenton From the Latin name Quintus, meaning "the fifth." In Roman times, often given to the fifth son in a family.

Quintin A variant spelling of Quentin. An ancient Roman personal name.

Quincy A variant form of Quentin.

Quinn A variant form of Quentin. Also, possibly from the Old English *cwen*, meaning "a queen" or "a companion."

R

Rain, Rainer, Rainier, Raines, Rains Probably from the British *rhen*, meaning "a lord," or from *rhann*, meaning "a portion."

Raleigh From the Old French *raale*, meaning "a field of wading birds."

Ralph From the Old Norse and Anglo-Saxon *rath*, meaning "counsel," and *ulfr*, meaning "a wolf," hence "courageous advice, fearless advisor."

Ramon A Spanish form of Raymond.

Ramsey From the Old English, meaning "ram's island." Ramsay is a variant spelling.

Randal, Randall From the Anglo-Saxon name Randwulf, derived from *rand*, meaning "a shield," and *wulf*, meaning "a wolf," connoting "superior protection." Akin to Ralph and Randolph.

Randell A variant spelling of Randall.

Randolph From the Anglo-Saxon name Randwulf. Akin to Ralph and Randal.

Raphael From the Hebrew, meaning "God has healed."

Ravi From the Hindi, meaning "sun."

Ray From the Old English *ree*, meaning "a stream."

Raymond A variant form of the Old French names Raimund and Raginmund, meaning "wise protection."

Razi From the Aramaic, meaning "my secret."

Red A nickname for redheaded people. Also, a variant spelling of Redd.

Redd From the Old English *hreod*, meaning "a reed."

Reece, Reese A Welsh form of the Old English *ree*, meaning "a stream."

Reed A variant spelling of Read. From the Old English *hreod*, meaning "a reed."

Reeves An Old English occupational name, meaning "a steward, one in charge of a manor."

Reggie A pet form of Reginald.

Reginald From the Old High German name Raganald, derived from *ragin*, meaning "wise, judicious," plus *ald* (akin to the Old English *eald*), meaning "old."

Regis From the Latin *rex*, meaning "kingly, regal."

Reid   A variant spelling of Read.

Reinhard, Reinhart   Variant German forms of Reynard.

Reinhold   A German form of Reginald.

Renaldo   An Italian form of Reginald.

Rene   A French name from the Latin *renatus* and *renovare*, meaning "to be reborn; to renew." St. Rene, also known as Renatus, was Bishop of Angers in the fifth century.

Reuben   From the Hebrew, meaning "behold—a son!" In the Bible, Jacob's first-born son from his wife Leah.

Reubin   A variant spelling of Reuben.

Rex   From the Latin, meaning "a king."

Reynard   From the Old High German name Reginhart, compounded from the Germanic *ragin*, meaning "wise," and *hart*, meaning "hard, bold, courageous."

Reynolds   A patronymic form of Reynold, meaning "the son of Reynold."

Rhett   A variant form of the Old English *ret*, from *rith*, meaning "a small stream."

Ricardo   A Spanish form of Richard.

Riccardo   An Italian form of Richard.

Richard   A French form of the Old High German name Richart, meaning "powerful, rich ruler."

Richardo   A Spanish form of Richard.

Richardson A patronymic form of Richard, meaning "the son of Richard."

Rick, Ricki, Rickie Pet forms of Richard.

Riley From the Dutch *ril* and the Low German *rille*, akin to the Old English *rith*, meaning "a small stream, a rivulet."

Rinaldo An Italian form of Reginald.

Rip From the Latin *ripa*, meaning "a river bank."

Ripley From the Latin and Old English, meaning "the meadow near the river's bank."

Rob A pet form of Robert.

Robert From the Old High German, meaning "bright fame" or "famous counsel."

Roberto The Spanish and Italian form of Robert.

Robin A form of Robert.

Robson A patronymic form, meaning "the son of Rob (Robert)."

Rocco A pet form of Richard.

Rock From the Old English *roche*, meaning "a rock."

Rod, Rodd From the British, meaning "open or cleared land."

Roderic, Roderick From the Old German, meaning "famous ruler."

Rodger, Rodgers Variant forms of Roger.

Rodney   From the Old English, meaning "the cleared land near the water."

Rodolph   A variant spelling of Rudolph.

Rodolpho   An Italian form of Rudolph.

Rodrigo   A Spanish and Italian form of Roderic.

Roger   An Old French form of the German name Ruodiger or Hrodger, akin to the Old English name Hrothgar. Hrothgar is from the Anglo-Saxon *hruod*, meaning "fame," plus *ger*, meaning "spear," hence "famous, noble warrior."

Roland   A French form of the Old High German, meaning "fame of the land." A legendary medieval figure famous for his strength.

Rolando   An Italian and Portuguese form of Roland.

Rolf, Rolfe   Pet forms of Rudolph.

Rolland   A variant spelling of Roland.

Roman   From the Latin name Romanus, meaning "a person from Rome."

Ron   A pet form of Ronald.

Ronald   The Scottish form of Reginald.

Roni   From the Hebrew, meaning "joy is mine."

Ross   From the British *rhos*, meaning "woods, meadow," or from the Norse *ross*, meaning "a headland," or from the Latin, meaning "a rose."

Roy   From the Old French, meaning "king." Also, from the Gaelic *rhu*, meaning "red." Also, possibly from the Old English *hry*, meaning "a thorn."

Royce   A variant form of Reece.

Ruben   A variant spelling of Reuben.

Rubens   A patronymic form of Reuben, meaning "son of Reuben."

Rubin   A variant spelling of Reuben.

Rudolph   From the Old High German name Hro-dulf, derived from *hruod*, meaning "fame," plus *wolf*, meaning "a wolf."

Russel, Russell   From the French *roux*, meaning "red."

Rusty   A nickname for a redheaded person.

Rutherford   From the Old English, meaning "the river crossing made of red stones."

Ryan   A short form of Bryan.

Ryder   A variant spelling of Rider, from the Middle English *ridden* and *ruden*, akin to the Old English *rydden*, meaning "to clear land." An occupational name, meaning "one who clears land, a farmer."

S

Sal, Sale   From the Latin *sal*, meaning "salt." Or, from the Old English *salh*, meaning "a willow." Sal is also a common pet form of Salvador.

Salem   The English form of the Hebrew *shalom*, meaning "peace."

Salvador From the Latin *salvare*, meaning "to be saved." Sal is a pet form.

Salvatore A variant spelling of Salvador.

Sam A pet form of Samuel.

Sammy A pet form of Samuel.

Samuel From the Hebrew, meaning "His name is God" or "God has heard."

Sander A pet form of Alexander.

Sanders A patronymic form, meaning "son of Sander."

Sandor A variant spelling of Sander, a pet form of Alexander.

Sanford From the Old English *sond*, meaning "sand," plus *ford*, meaning "a crossing," hence "the sandy river crossing."

Santo, Santos Spanish forms of the Latin *sanctus*, meaning "saint."

Saul From the Hebrew, meaning "borrowed."

Sawyer From the Middle English *sawier*, meaning "one who works with a saw." An occupational name used by woodcutters and cabinet makers.

Schubert From the German, meaning "bright protector."

Scot, Scott From Scoti, a Late Latin name for a tribe of people in North Britain. Scottie, and Scotty are pet forms.

Sean An Irish form of John.

Seargent A variant spelling of Sargent.

Sebastian From the Greek, meaning "venerable."

Segel From the Hebrew *segula,* meaning "treasure."

Selden, Seldon From the Middle English, meaning "rare, strange."

Selwyn From the Old English *sel (saelig),* meaning "holy," plus *wyn,* meaning "friend," hence "holy friend." A common name in Wales.

Serge, Sergei From the Old French *sergant* and the Latin *servire,* meaning "to serve."

Sergi, Sergio Variant Italian forms of Serge.

Seth From the Hebrew, meaning either "garment" or "appointed," or from the Syriac, meaning "appearance."

Seward From the Anglo-Saxon, meaning "defender of the sea coast."

Seymour From the Old English *sae,* meaning "sea," and *mor,* meaning "marsh, marshy, wild land," hence "marshy land near the sea." Akin to Maurice.

Shane A variant form of the Gaelic Sean.

Shanen A variant spelling of Shanon.

Shannon, Shanon Variant forms of Sean. Or Shaanan.

Sharon A masculine as well as feminine form. From the Hebrew *yashar,* meaning "a plain, a flat area."

Shaw   From the Old English *scaega*, meaning "a thicket, a grove."

Shawn   A variant spelling of Sean.

Shel   A pet form of Shelley or Shelby.

Shelby   From the Anglo-Saxon, meaning "a sheltered town."

Sheldon   From the Old English *scyld*, meaning "a hill," hence "protected hill."

Shelley, Shelly   From the Old English, meaning "island of shells."

Shelton   From the Old English, meaning "protected town." Akin to Sheldon.

Shem   From the Hebrew, meaning "name." In the Bible, the oldest of Noah's sons. Shammai is a variant form.

Shepley   From the Old English *sceap*, meaning "a sheep meadow."

Sheridan   From the Old English, meaning "master of the shire, head of the district." Akin to Sherwood.

Sherill   From the Old English *scire*, meaning "a shire," plus *hyl*, meaning "a hill," hence "the hill in the district (shire)" or "the hilly shire." Akin to Sherwood. Sherrill is a variant spelling.

Sherman   From the Old English, meaning "a servant (or resident) of the shire (district)." Akin to Sherwood. Also, an occupational name, meaning "one who shears sheep."

Sherry   A pet form of Sherman or Sherwood.

Sherwin From the Old English, meaning "a friend, a member of the shire." Akin to Sherwood.

Sherwood From the Old English *scyre, scir, scire*, meaning "a shire, a county, an official district," plus *wood*, meaning "a wooded area, a forest."

Shirley Used occasionally as a masculine name.

Sholom A variant spelling of Shalom, from the Hebrew, meaning "peace."

Sidney A contracted form of Saint Denys. Derived from Dionysius, the Greek god of wine, drama, and fruitfulness. Sydney is a variant spelling.

Silas A Latin form of the Aramaic and Hebrew *sha-ol*, meaning "to ask, to borrow."

Silvester A variant spelling of Sylvester.

Simeon A Greek and Latin form of the Hebrew Shimon, from *shama*, meaning "he heard."

Simon A variant spelling of Simeon.

Simpson A patronymic form, meaning "son of Simon."

Sims A patronymic form, meaning "son of Simon."

Sinclair From the Latin, meaning "a clear sign." Also, may be a contracted form of Saint Claire.

Skee From the Old Norse *skeyti*, meaning "a projectile." Sky is a variant form.

Skip A pet form of Skipper.

Skipper   From the Middle Dutch *schipper*, meaning "one who captains a ship."

Sloan   From the Celtic, meaning "warrior."

Sly   A pet form of Sylvester.

Snowy   A nickname for a white-complexioned person.

Sol   A pet form of Solomon.

Solomon   From the Hebrew *shalom*, meaning "peace."

Sonny   A popular nickname, meaning "son" or "boy."

Soren   Origin uncertain. Possibly from Thor, the Norse god of war.

Speed   From the Old English *spaed*, meaning "wealth, power, success."

Spencer   From the Middle English *spenser*, meaning "steward, administrator, butler."

Spike   From the Middle English *spik* and the Latin *spica*, meaning "an ear of grain."

Spiro   From the Latin *spirate*, meaning "to breathe."

Squire   From the Old French *esquier*, meaning "a young man of high birth serving as an attendant to nobility."

Stacey, Stacy   From the Latin, meaning "firmly established."

Stafford   From the Old English *staef* plus *ford*, meaning "a pole with which to ford (cross) a river."

Stan A pet form of many names, primarily Stanley.

Stanford From the Old English, meaning "a stone river crossing."

Stanley From the Old English *stan* plus *lea*, meaning "a stony meadow." Akin to Stansfield. Stan is a pet form.

Stansfield From the Old English *stans* plus *feld*, meaning "a field of stone." Akin to Stanley.

Stanton From the Old English, meaning "the town near the stony field." Akin to Stanley and Stansfield.

Stefan A variant spelling of the German Stephan.

Stephan The German form of Stephen.

Stephen From the Greek *stephanos*, meaning "a crown." In the Bible, one of the seven chosen to assist the apostles. A popular saint name.

Sterling From the Middle English *sterlinge*, meaning "a silver penny." Also, possibly from the Old English *staerlinc*, meaning "a starling (bird)."

Steven An English variant form of Stuart.

Stewart A variant form of Stuart.

Stirling A variant spelling of Sterling.

Stockton From the Old English *stoc, stocc*, akin to the German *stock*, meaning "the trunk of a tree," hence "the town *(ton)* near the tree trunk."

Storm From the Old English, meaning "a storm."

Stu A pet form of Stuart.

Stuart From the Old English, meaning "a steward, a keeper of an estate."

Studs From the Old English *studu,* meaning "a post, a pillar," and later, "a house."

Styles From the Latin name Stilus, meaning "a pointed instrument for writing," hence "one who writes." Probably an occupational name.

Sullivan From the Old English *sul* or *syl,* meaning "a plough," plus the British *ban,* meaning "high, a high place," hence "a plowed plot on the hill."

Sully From the Old French, meaning "stain, tarnish."

Sumner From the Latin, meaning "one who summons or calls."

Sunny A nickname which has become an independent name. Or, from the Old English *sunna,* meaning "the sun."

Sutton From the Old English *suth,* meaning "the town to the south."

Sven From Svealand, the earliest name of the area in which Sweden is located, named for the Swedish tribe called Svear.

Swen A variant form of Sven.

Sy A pet form of Seymour and Sylvan.

Sydney A variant spelling of Sidney.

Sylvan A variant form of Silvanus, meaning "forest, woods."

Sylvester A variant form of Silvanus.

T

Tab   A pet form of David. Taffy is a variant form.

Tad   A pet form of Thaddeus.

Taft   From the British *taf,* meaning "a river."

Talbot   From the Old English, meaning "Botolph's River."

Taldon   From the Celtic and the Old English, meaning "the lake near the hill (don)."

Tarver   From the Old English *tor,* meaning "a tower, a hill." Or, from the Old English *tawer,* meaning "a leader."

Tate   From the Old English *teotha,* meaning "a tenth, a tithing." Used also as a feminine name.

Taylor   An Old English occupational name, meaning "tailor."

Ted, Teddy   Pet forms of Theodore.

Teodoro   A Spanish form of Theodore.

Terence, Terrence   From the Latin, meaning "tender, good, gracious." Terentius was an early Roman family name.

Terrance   A variant spelling of Terence.

Terrel   Probably a variant form of Terence.

Terris   Probably a patronymic form of Terry, meaning "son of Terry."

Terry   A pet form of Terence.

Terryal   A variant form of Terry.

Tex   A nickname for a Texan.

Thad   A pet form of Thadeus.

Thadeus, Thaddeus   From the Greek, meaning "gift of God."

Thadford   From the Old English, meaning "Thad's (Thadeus's) crossing (ford)."

Thane   From the Middle English *thayne*, meaning "to engender, to beget," hence "a freeborn man."

Tharon   A variant spelling of Theron.

Thayer   A name meaning "of the nation's army."

Theo   A pet form of Theodore.

Theodor, Theodore   From the Greek *theos*, meaning "God," plus *doron*, meaning "gift," hence "divine gift."

Theodric   From the Old German name Thiudoricus. Compounded of *theuda*, meaning "folk, people," and *ric*, meaning "ruler," hence "ruler of the people."

Theron   From the Greek, meaning "a hunter." Tharon is a variant spelling.

Thom   A pet form of Thomas.

Thomas   From the Hebrew and Aramaic *t'ome*, meaning "a twin." Also, from the Phoenecian, meaning "sun god."

Thompson A patronymic form, meaning "son of Thomas." Commonly used as a surname.

Thornton From the Anglo-Saxon, meaning "from the thorny place (town)."

Thruston A variant form of Thurston.

Thurman From the Norse and Old English, meaning "servant of Thor."

Thurstan, Thurston From the Scandinavian, compounded of Thor and *stan (stein)*, meaning "stone," hence "Thor's stone or jewel."

Tibon From the Hebrew, meaning "a naturalist, a student of nature." Tivon is a variant form.

Tibor From the Old English *tiber*, meaning "holy, a holy place, an altar."

Tilden From the Anglo-Saxon, meaning "a tilled or fertile valley."

Tim A pet form of Timothy.

Timmy A pet form of Timothy.

Timothy From the Greek, meaning "to honor God." Thaddeus is an Old Greek variant.

Tino An Italian suffix meaning "small." Also, a pet form of Tony.

Tip A nickname for Thomas.

Tobiah From the Hebrew, meaning "the Lord is my good."

Tobias The Greek form of Tobiah.

Tobey A variant spelling of Toby.

Tobin   A pet form of Tobiah.

Toby   A pet form of Tobiah.

Tod, Todd   From the Old English *tod*, meaning "fox." Also, a pet form of Robert, and a variant spelling of Tad.

Toller   From the Old English *toll*, meaning "one who levies or collects taxes."

Tom   A pet form of Thomas.

Tomas   A variant form of Thomas.

Tomie, Tommie   Pet forms of Thomas.

Tommy   A pet form of Thomas.

Toney   A variant spelling of Tony.

Toni, Tony   Pet forms of Anthony.

Topper   From the British *top*, meaning "a hill."

Torbert   From the Anglo-Saxon *tor*, meaning "hill," and *bert*, meaning "bright."

Torrance, Torrence   An Irish form of Terence.

Torrey   A pet form of Torrance.

Townsend   From the Anglo-Saxon, meaning "the end of town."

Tracey, Tracy   From the Old French, meaning "path" or "road."

Travis   From the Latin and French, meaning "crossroads."

Trenton   From the French *trente*, meaning "thirty."

Treva A variant form of the French *trier*, meaning "to assign priorities." Akin to Trevor.

Trevor From the Celtic, meaning "prudent." Akin to Treva.

Trini From the Latin *trinitas*, meaning "three, trinity."

Troy From the Greek name Troia, a form of Tros, father of Ilos in Homer's *The Illiad*. Also, from the British *wye*, meaning "water."

Truman From the Anglo-Saxon, meaning "a true, loyal man."

Tucker An English occupational name, meaning "one who cleans and thickens cloth."

Turner From the Latin, meaning "a worker with a lathe."

Ty From the British, meaning "a house." Twy is a variant form.

Tyler From the British, possibly meaning "a house builder." Ty is a pet form.

Tyron, Tyrone From the Latin *tiro*, meaning "a young soldier."

Tyrus From the Latin Tyrus, meaning "a person from the Tyre," a seaport in southwestern Lebanon. Ty is a pet form.

U

Ulises A variant spelling of Ulysses.

Ulric, Ulrich, Ulrick From the Danish, meaning "a wolf."

Ulysses   The Latin name of Odysseus, the hero of Homer's *Odyssey*, a king of Ithaca and one of the Greek heroes of the Trojan War.

Umberto   From the Italian *terra d'ombre*, meaning "shade (color) of the earth."

Upton   From the Anglo-Saxon, meaning "the upper town."

Urban   From the Latin *urbanus*, meaning "a city."

Uri   From the Hebrew, meaning "my light."

Uriah   From the Hebrew, meaning "God is my light."

V

Vail   From the Latin *vallis*, meaning "the valley."

Val   The French form of Vail.

Van   The Dutch form of the German *von*, meaning "from" a particular city. Akin to the French *de*.

Vance   A form of the British name Vans, from *fannau*, meaning "high, high places."

Vander   Probably from the Dutch, meaning "of the" or "from the," a prefix to many place-names.

Varner   Probably a variant form of Werner.

Vaughan, Vaughn   From the Celtic, meaning "small."

Vern   From the British *gwern*, meaning "an alder tree." Or, a pet form of Vernon.

Verne   A variant spelling of Vern.

Vernon From the Latin *vernalis* and *vernus*, meaning "belonging to spring," hence "flourishing." Also, from the British *gwern*, meaning "an alder tree."

Vic A pet form of Victor.

Vicente From the Latin *viceni*, meaning "twenty."

Victor From the Latin *vincere*, meaning "victor, conqueror."

Vidal A variant form of Vida, from the Latin *vita*, meaning "life."

Vince A pet form of Vincent.

Vincent From the Latin *vincere*, meaning "victor, conqueror."

Vinson A patronymic form, meaning "the son of Vincent."

Virgil From the Latin, meaning "strong, flourishing." Vergil is a variant spelling.

Viron From the Latin *ver*, meaning "spring," hence "flourishing."

Vito A pet form of Vittorio, the Italian form of Victor.

Wade From the Old English *waden*, meaning "to wade."

Walden From the Old English *waeld*, meaning "woods."

Waldo, Waldron From the Old English *walda*, meaning "a ruler."

Walker   From the Old English occupational name for "one who cleans and thickens cloth."

Wallace   From the Anglo-French name Waleis and the Middle English Walisc, meaning "a foreigner, stranger."

Wally   A pet form of Walter or Wallace.

Walter   From the Old English *weald*, meaning "woods." Also, from the Old French *waldan*, meaning "to wield, to rule," plus *heri, hari*, meaning "army," hence "a general."

Walton   From the Old English *gwal*, meaning "a wall, a fortification," plus *ton*, meaning "town," hence "the fortified town."

Ward   From the Old English *weardian*, meaning "to guard; a guardian."

Warner   A variant form of Warren.

Warren   From the Middle English *wareine* and the Old French *warir*, meaning "to preserve." Also, "an enclosure (for rabbits)."

Wayland   From the Old English *waeg*, meaning "way, road," hence "the land near the highway."

Wayne   From the British *waun*, meaning "a meadow."

Webster   From the Old English *wiba*, meaning "a weaver." Webb is a pet form.

Wellington   From the Old English, meaning "the town near the water" or "the town near the willow trees."

Wendel, Wendell   From the British and Old English, meaning "a good dale or valley."

Werner A variant form of Warren.

Wesley From the Old English, meaning "the west meadow."

Westcott From the Old English, meaning "the cottage in the western field."

Weston From the Old English *waest-town*, meaning "house built on waste land," or from "west town," the town to the west.

Wharton From the Old English *waeg-faru*, meaning "a way by the water."

Whitney From the Old English, meaning "a small piece of land near the water *(ey).*" Akin to Whitley and Whittaker.

Wilbur, Wilburn Variant forms of Wilber, from the Old English *gwal*, meaning "wall, fortification," plus *beorht*, meaning "bright, respected," hence "secure fortification."

Wiley, Wylie From the Old English, meaning "wiillow field; a meadow of willows."

Wilfred, Wilfrid, Wilfried From the Old English name Wilfrith, derived from *willa*, meaning "wish, desire," plus *frith*, meaning "peace," hence "hope for peace."

William A variant form of the Old French name Willaume and the Old High German Willehelm. From the Old High German *willeo*, meaning "will, desire," and *helm*, meaning "protection," hence "resolute protector."

Willis A patronymic form, meaning "son of William."

Wilson A patronymic form, meaning "the son of William."

Winston From the Old English *win*, meaning "victory," plus *ton*, meaning "town," hence "victory town."

Winthrop From the Old English *win*, meaning "victory," plus *throp*, meaning "crossroads," hence "victory at the crossroads."

Wood From the Anglo-Saxon, meaning "from the wooded area (forest)."

Woodrow From the Old English, meaning "wooded hedge."

Wright From the Old English, meaning "an artisan, a worker."

Wyatt, Wyatte From the British *gwy*, meaning "water."

Wycliffe A variant form of Wyck, meaning "village near the cliff."

X

Xavier From the Arabic, meaning "bright."

Y

Yale From the German, meaning "one who pays or produces." Also, from the Old English *eald*, meaning "old."

Yancy A corruption of the French word for "Englishman," which evolved into Yankee. Also, a variant form of the Danish name Jan (John).

Yardley   From the Old English *geard,* meaning "an enclosure, a yard."

Yaron   From the Hebrew, meaning "He will sing."

Yates   From the British *iat,* meaning "a gate."

Yavin   From the Hebrew, meaning "He will understand."

Yogi   A nickname. Also, from the Sanskrit *yogin,* meaning "a person who practices yoga."

York   A variant form of Yorick, probably a Danish variant form of George.

Yosef, Yoseph   Hebraic forms of Joseph.

Zachariah, Zacharias   Variant forms of Zechariah.

Zachary   A variant form of Zechariah.

Zane   A variant form of Zan, from the Italian *zanni,* meaning "a clown."

Zebulon   A variant spelling of Zebulun.

Zebulun   From the Hebrew, meaning "to exalt, to honor" or "a lofty house."

Zechariah   From the Hebrew, meaning "the remembrance of the Lord."

Zecharias   A Greek form of Zechariah.

Zedekiah   From the Hebrew, meaning "God is righteousness."

Zeeb   A variant spelling of Zev. In the Bible, a prince of Midian.

Zeev   A variant spelling of Zev.

Zev   From the Hebrew *z'ayv*, meaning "a wolf."

Feminine
Names

A

Abby   A pet form of Abigail.

Abigail   The anglicized form of the Hebrew name Avigayil, meaning "father of joy."

Ada, Adah From the Hebrew, meaning "adorned, beautiful."

Adaline   A pet form of Adelaide.

Adda, Addie   Pet forms of Adelaide.

Addison   A patronymic form of the pet form of Adelaide, meaning "Addie's son."

Adela, Adella   Variant forms of Adelaide.

Adelaide   A French form of the German name Adelheid, meaning "of noble birth."

Adele, Adelle   Variant forms of Adelaide.

Adena   From the Hebrew and Greek, meaning "noble" or "adorned."

Adie   From the Hebrew, meaning "ornament."

Adira   From the Hebrew, meaning "mighty, strong."

Adrea, Adria   Variant spellings of Adrienne.

Adrien, Adrienne   French forms derived from the Greek, meaning "a girl from Adria." Adria and Adrian are variant forms.

Agatha   From the Greek and Latin, meaning "good."

Agnes   From the Greek and Latin, meaning "lamb," symbolizing purity and chastity.

Aida   From the Latin and Old French, meaning "to help."

Aileen, Ailene   From the Greek, meaning "light." Akin to Helen.

Aimee   The French form of the Latin *amor*, meaning "love."

Alaina, Alaine   Feminine forms of Alan. May also be variant forms of Helen.

Alana, Alanna   A feminine form of Alan.

Alayne   A variant spelling of Alaine.

Alcina   Probably a feminine form of the Greek Alcindor and Alcander, meaning "manly."

Alda   From the Old German, meaning "old." Aude is a variant form used in twelfth-century England.

Aleda   A variant form of Alda.

Alena   A Russian form of Helen.

Alene   A variant form of Arlene or Eileen.

Alessandra An Italian variant form of Alexandra.

Alethea, Alethia, Alithea From the Greek, meaning "truth." A seventeenth-century name that came to England through Spain.

Alexa A variant form of Alexandra.

Alexandra, Alexandria, Alexandrina Feminine forms of the Greek name Alexander, meaning "protector of man."

Alexina, Alexine Pet forms of Alexandra.

Alexis A variant form of Alexandra.

Ali A pet form of Alice or Alison.

Alice From the Middle English names Alys and Aeleis, which evolved from the Old French Aliz and Aaliz. Originally the Old High German name Adelheidis, akin to Adelaide, meaning "of noble birth."

Alicia A variant form of Alice.

Alida, Alidia From the Greek, meaning "beautifully dressed."

Alison A matronymic form, meaning "the son of Alice."

Aliza, Alizah From the Hebrew, meaning "joy, joyous one."

Allie A pet form of Alice or Allison.

Allison A matronymic form, meaning "son of Alice."

Allissa A variant form of Alice.

Allyn   A variant spelling of Allen. Primarily a masculine name.

Althea   From the Greek and Latin, meaning "to heal" or "healer."

Alyce   A variant spelling of Alice.

Alyson   A variant spelling of Alison.

Amalia, Amaliah   From the Hebrew, meaning "the work of the Lord."

Amanda   From the Latin, meaning "worthy of love." Mandy is a pet form.

Amelia   From the Hebrew and Latin *amal*, meaning "work."

Ami, Amie   Variant spellings of Amy.

Amina, Amine   From the Hebrew and Arabic *amin*, meaning "trusted, faithful." Feminine forms of Amin.

Amira   From the Hebrew, meaning "speech, utterance."

Amy   The French form of the Latin *amor*, meaning "love."

Anastasia   From the Greek, meaning "resurrection."

Andrea   From the Greek, meaning "valiant, strong, courageous."

Anett   A variant spelling of Annette.

Angela   From the Middle Latin name Angelica and the Latin *angelicus*, meaning "angelic."

Angelica   The Latin form of Angela.

Angelina, Angeline   Pet forms of Angela.

Anita   The Spanish form of Anna.

Ann   A variant spelling of Anne.

Anna   The Greek form of the Hebrew name Hannah, meaning "gracious."

Annabel   A variant form of Annabella.

Annabella, Annabelle   Compounded of Anna and Bella, meaning "gracious and beautiful."

Anne   A French form of the Hebrew name Hannah, meaning "gracious."

Annemarie   A compound of Anne and Marie.

Annette   A French form of Anna.

Annie   Usually a pet form of Ann, Anna, or Hannah.

Anthea   From the Greek, meaning "flowery."

Antoinette   The feminine French form of Antony.

Antonette   A variant form of Antoinette.

April   From the Latin, meaning "to open," symbolic of springtime. April was used by the early Romans as the name of the second month of the year.

Arda, Ardah   From the Hebrew, meaning "bronze, bronzed." Also, a variant form of the Hebrew month Adar.

Aretha   A variant form of Arethusa, in Greek mythology, a woodland nymph who was changed into a stream by Artemis. Also, a variety of orchid.

Ariel, Ariela, Ariella, Arielle   From the Hebrew, meaning "lioness of God."

Aritha   A variant form of Aretha.

Arla   A variant form of Arlene. Or, a short form of Carla.

Arlana   A pet form of Arlene.

Arleen   A variant spelling of Arlene.

Arlene   A variant spelling of Arline. Or, from the Celtic, meaning "a pledge, an oath."

Arleta, Arlette   Pet forms of Arlene or Arline.

Arline, Arlyne   From the German, meaning "girl." Or, a form of Adeline.

Ashira   From the Hebrew, meaning "wealthy."

Astera, Asteria   From the Greek *aster*, meaning "a star."

Athalia   From the Hebrew, meaning "God is exalted."

Athena   From the Greek, meaning "wisdom."

Atira   From the Hebrew, meaning "a prayer."

Audra   A variant form of Audrey.

Audrey   From the Old English, meaning "noble strength."

Aurelia   The feminine form of the Latin name Aurelius, meaning "gold."

Aurora   From the Latin, meaning "dawn."

Ava   From the Latin name Avis, meaning "bird." Or, a short form of Avalon.

Avalon, Avallon   French forms of the Middle Latin name Avallonis, meaning "island." In Celtic mythology, the Isle of the Dead, an island in paradise where King Arthur and other heroes went after death.

Avella   A pet form of Aveline, from the French, meaning "hazel nut."

Bab, Babette   Pet forms of Elizabeth and Barbara.

Bambi   A pet form of Bambalina, the diminutive form of the Italian *bambo*, meaning "child, childish."

Bara, Barra   From the Hebrew, meaning "to choose."

Barbara   From the Roman name Barbari, derived from the Latin *barbarus*, meaning "strange, foreign."

Barbi, Barbo   Pet forms of Barbara.

Bari, Barrie   Feminine forms of Barrie.

Bea, Beah   Pet forms of Beatrice.

Beatrice   From the Latin *beatrix*, meaning "one who brings happiness, a blessing."

Beckie, Becky   Popular pet forms of Rebecca.

Belinda   From the Latin *bel* and *bellus*, meaning "beautiful," and the Old Norse *linnr*, meaning "snake."

Bell   A pet form of Isabel used since the thirteenth century.

Bella, Belle   Short forms of Isabella.

Berenice   From the Greek, meaning "bringer of victory."

Bernadette   From the French and German, meaning "bold as a bear."

Berneta, Bernetta, Bernette   Variant forms of Bernadette.

Bernice, Berniece   Variant forms of Berenice.

Beryl   From the Greek and Sanskrit, meaning "a precious stone."

Bess, Bessie   Pet forms of Elizabeth.

Beth   A short form of Elizabeth.

Betsey, Betsy   Pet forms of Elizabeth.

Bette   A pet form of Elizabeth.

Betty   A popular pet form of Elizabeth.

Beverley, Beverly   From the Old English, meaning "a beaver's meadow."

Bianca   The Italian of the Spanish *blanc*, meaning "white."

Bibi   From the French *beubelot*, hence the English *bibelot*, meaning "a bauble, a toy."

Billie   A feminine form of William.

Billie Jean   A compounded name of Billie and Jean.

Birgit, Birgitta   Variant forms of Bridget.

Blair   From the Gaelic, meaning "field" or "battle."

Blanca   The Spanish form of the French *blanc*, meaning "white."

Blanche   From the Old French *blanc*, meaning "white."

Blaze   From the Old English, meaning "a flame" or "a mark made on a tree" to mark a trail in a forest.

Blythe   From the Anglo-Saxon, meaning "happy."

Bobette   A pet form of Barbara and Roberta.

Bonnie, Bonny   From the Latin *bonus* and the French *bon*, meaning "good" or "pretty."

Brenda   A feminine form of Brandon and Brendan.

Breyette   A pet form of Bree, from the Middle English *bre*, meaning "a broth."

Bridget   A variant form of Brighid. From the Celtic, meaning "strong, lofty." In medieval folklore, Brighid was a Celtic fire goddess.

Bridgit   A variant spelling of Bridget.

Brigid, Brigit, Brigitte   Variant forms of Bridget.

Brina   From the Slavic, meaning "protector." Akin to Brian.

Brook, Brooke   From the Old English *broc* and Middle English *brok,* meaning "to break out," as a stream of water.

C

Caasi   A variant form of Catherine or Cassandra.

Cadette   A pet form of the French name Cadice, meaning "little chief."

Cadice   From the French *cad,* meaning "a chief."

Caitlin   A variant Welsh form of Catherine.

Callan   From the Middle English *callen* and the Old Norse *kalla,* meaning "to scream, to shriek."

Cameo   The Italian form of the Latin, meaning "a carving."

Camilla   A variant form of Camille.

Camille   From the Latin, meaning "a virgin of unblemished character."

Candace   From the Greek, meaning "fire-white" or "incandescent."

Candia   Port city of Crete, now called Heraklion.

Candice   A variant spelling of Candace.

Candida, Candide   Variant forms of Candace.

Candyce   A pet form of Candace.

Caprice   From the Latin, meaning "a head with bristling hair; a hedgehog." Or, from the French, meaning "erratic."

Cara   A short form of Charlotte and Caroline.

Caren   A variant form of Catherine.

Carey   A pet form of Caroline.

Carita   From the Latin *caritas*, meaning "charity."

Carla   The feminine form of Carl or Charles; a short form of Caroline.

Carley   A variant form of Carla and Caroline.

Carlia   A pet form of Carla and Caroline.

Carlin   A variant form of Caroline.

Carlita   An Italian pet form of Carla and Caroline.

Carlotta   The Italian form of Charlotte.

Carly   A pet form of Carla and Caroline.

Carmen   The Spanish form of Carma or Carmel, from the Hebrew *kerom*, meaning "a vineyard."

Carol, Carola, Carole   From the Gaelic, meaning "melody, song."

Caroleen   A variant form of Caroline.

Caroline   A French form of the Middle Latin name Carolus and the English name Charles, meaning "strong, virile."

Carolyn   A variant spelling of Caroline.

Carrie   A pet form of Caroline.

Carry   A pet form of Caroline.

Cass   A pet form of Cassandra.

Cassandra   From the Greek, referring to "one whose warnings are ignored."

Cassia   From the Greek *kasia*, meaning "a type of cinnamon."

Cassie   A pet form of Catherine.

Catherine   From the Greek *katharos*, meaning "pure, unsullied."

Cathleen   An Irish form of Catherine.

Cathryn   A variant spelling of Catherine.

Cecelia   From the Latin name Caecilia, the feminine form of the Roman family name Caecilius, meaning "a member of the (legless) lizard family." Also, from the Latin *caecus*, meaning "blind."

Cecely   A variant form of Cecelia.

Cecily   A variant form of Cecelia.

Celeste   From the Latin, meaning "heavenly."

Celina   A variant form of Celeste.

Chandra   From the Sanskrit, meaning "illustrious" or "eminent."

Chantal   A French form of the Latin *cantus*, meaning "a song."

Charis, Charissa From the Greek, meaning "grace, beauty, kindness."

Charity From the Latin *caritas,* meaning "esteem, affection."

Charlena, Charlene Variant forms of Caroline and Charlotte.

Charlinda A name invented by combining *Charles* and *Linda.*

Charlotte The French pet form of Charlot, a feminine form of Charles.

Charmain, Charmaine From the Latin *carmen,* meaning "to sing."

Charo A variant form of Caroline.

Chelsea From the Anglo-Saxon, meaning "a port of ships."

Cher A pet form of Cheryl.

Cheri, Cherie Pet forms of Cheryl.

Cherry A pet form of Cheryl.

Cheryl, Cheryle From the French, meaning "beloved."

Chloe From the Greek, meaning "blooming, verdant."

Chrissie A pet form of Christine.

Christa A pet form of Christabel. Compounded of *Christ* and *bella,* meaning "handsome Christ."

Christal A Scotch form of Christian or Christopher.

Christel   A variant spelling of Christal.

Christie   A pet form of Christine, meaning "a Christian."

Christina   A variant form of Christine.

Christine   A variant form of Christiana, the feminine form of Christianus, meaning "a Christian, a believer in Jesus as the anointed one."

Christy   A pet form of Christine.

Chrystal   A variant spelling of Crystal.

Cicely, Cicily   Variant forms of Cecilia.

Cindy   A pet form of Cynthia.

Civia   A form of the Hebrew *tzevi (tzvi)*, meaning "a deer."

Claira   A variant form of Clara.

Claire   The French form of Clara.

Clara   From the Latin *clarus*, meaning "clear, bright."

Clare   A variant form of Clara.

Clarette   A variant form of Clara.

Clarice   A variant spelling of Clarisse.

Clarissa   An Italian form of Clara.

Clarisse   The French form of Clarissa.

Claudette   A French pet form of Claudia.

Claudia   From the Latin, meaning "lame." Gladys is the Welsh form.

Claudine   A French pet form of Claudia, popular in Switzerland.

Cleo   A variant spelling of Clio.

Clio   From the Greek, meaning "to celebrate, to glorify."

Cloris   A variant spelling of Chloris, from the Greek, meaning "blooming, verdant."

Clove   From the Latin *clavus*, meaning "a nail."

Colette   From the Latin, meaning "victorious."

Colleen   From the Irish *cailun*, meaning "girl."

Collice   Probably a variant form of Colleen.

Connie   A pet form of Constance.

Constance   From the Latin *constantia*, meaning "constant, faithful."

Cora   From the Greek *kore*, meaning "maiden."

Coral   From the Greek *korallion*, meaning "a small stone," usually red in color.

Coralie   A variant form of Cora.

Cordelia   From the Celtic, meaning "daughter of the sea."

Cordelle   The French diminutive form of *corde*, meaning "a rope."

Coretta, Corette   Pet forms of Cora.

Corey   From the Gaelic, meaning "a ravine, a deep hollow."

Cori, Corie   Pet forms of Cora.

Corinne   A French form of Cora.

Cornelia   From the Latin *cornus*, meaning "a cornell tree."

Courtney   From the Old French, meaning "one who frequents the king's court." Also a masculine form when spelled Courtnay.

Crisann   A name invented by combining Christine and Ann.

Crissie   A pet form of Christine.

Crystal   From the Greek, meaning "a clear, brilliant glass."

Cybil, Cybill   From the Latin, meaning "soothsayer."

Cyd   From the Old English, meaning "a public hill."

Cyndi Lu   A nickname for Lucinda.

Cyndy   A pet form of Cynthia.

Cynthia   From the Greek *kynthos*, meaning "from the cynthus."

Dafna, Dafne   Variant forms of the Greek name Daphne.

Dahlia   A perennial plant with large flower heads named for eighteenth-century Swedish botanist A. Dahl.

Daisy   From the Middle English *daies ie,* meaning "day's eye." A common nickname for Margaret, derived from St. Margherita of Italy, who took the daisy (flower) as her symbol.

Dale   From the Anglo-Saxon, meaning "a dweller in a vale between hills."

Dalia   From the Hebrew, meaning either "a branch, a bough" or "to draw water."

Dama   From the Latin *domina,* meaning "a lady."

Dana   From the Latin, meaning "bright, pure as day," or from the Hebrew, meaning "to judge."

Dania   A feminine form of Dan and Daniel.

Danice   A feminine form of Dan and Daniel.

Daniela, Daniella, Daniele, Danielle   Feminine forms of Daniel, meaning "God is my judge."

Dantia   A feminine form of Dante.

Daphna   A variant spelling of Daphne.

Daphne   From the Greek, meaning "the laurel or bay tree."

Dara From the Middle English *dar* and the Old English *dear*, meaning "to dare," hence "a courageous person." Dare is a variant form.

Darcie, Darcy From the Celtic, meaning "dark."

Daria The feminine form of the Persian name Darius, meaning "a king."

Darla From the Middle English *sereling*, meaning "dear, a loved one."

Darleen, Darlene, Darline From the Anglo-Saxon, meaning "dearly beloved."

Daryl From the Old English *deorling*, meaning "dear, beloved."

Dasi, Dassi Pet forms of Hadassah.

Dasia, Datia From the Hebrew, meaning "the law of the Lord."

Davalyn An invented name, compounded of David and Lyn.

Davi, Davida Variant forms of the masculine form David.

Dawn From the Old Norse *dagan*, meaning "dawn."

Daya, Dayah From the Hebrew, meaning "a bird."

Deanna, Deanne Variant spellings of Diane or Dinah.

Deannie A pet form of Deanna.

Debbi, Debbie Pet forms of Deborah.

Debby   A pet form of Deborah.

Deborah   From the Hebrew, meaning "a bee," or "to speak kind words."

Dee   From the British *du-wy*, meaning "dark water."

Deena   A variant Hebrew form of Dinah.

Deirdre   From the Middle Irish *der*, meaning "a young girl."

Delia   The Latin feminine form of Delius, meaning "an inhabitant of Delos" (a small island in the Aegean, the legendary birthplace of Artemis and Apollo).

Delila, Delilah   From the Hebrew, meaning either "poor" or "hair."

Dell, Della, Delle   Pet forms of Adele and Adeline.

Delpha   From the Greek *delphis*, meaning "a dolphin."

Delphinia   From the Greek *delphis*, meaning "a dolphin."

Delta   From the Greek *delta* and the Hebrew *daled* (*dalet*), the fourth letter of both alphabets, meaning "a door."

Dena   A variant Hebrew form of Dinah.

Deney   A pet form of Denise.

Deniece, Deniese   A variant spelling of Denise.

Denise   A feminine form of Denis, derived from Dionysius, the Greek god of wine and drama.

Denna   From the Anglo-Saxon, meaning "glen, valley."

Desire, Desiree   From the Old French *desirer*, meaning "to look to the stars, to crave."

Devlynn   An invented name in which a "D" was added to Evelyn, and the second "e" dropped and an "n" added.

Devon   A first name derived from the place-name on the English Channel.

Devora, Devorah   Variant Hebraic forms of Deborah.

Devra   A variant form of Deborah.

Di   A pet form of Diana.

Diana   From the Latin *dius*, meaning "divine." In Roman mythology, the virgin goddess of the moon and of hunting.

Diandra   From the Greek, meaning "a flower with two stamens."

Diane   The French form of Diana.

Dicie   From the British, meaning "risky, hazardous."

Diedra   A variant form of Dierdre.

Dierdre   A variant spelling of Deirdre, from the Middle Irish *der*, meaning "a young girl."

Dilli   A variant form of Dillian.

Dillian   From the British *delw*, meaning "an idol."

Dilys   From the Welsh, meaning "genuine."

Dimitra The feminine form of Demetrius.

Dinah From the Hebrew, meaning "judgement."

Dione, Dionne The Greek form of the Latin name Diana.

Ditza, Ditzah From the Hebrew, meaning "joy."

Dixie From the Old English *dix*, meaning "a dike (dyke), a wall."

Dodi, Dodie From the Hebrew, meaning "my friend, my beloved."

Dollie A variant spelling of Dolly.

Dolly A variant form of Dorothy.

Dolores From the Latin and Spanish, meaning "lady of sorrows."

Dominica The feminine form of Dominic, meaning "belonging to the Lord."

Dominique The French form of Dominica.

Donna An Italian form of the Latin *domina*, meaning "lady, madam," a title of respect.

Dora A variant form of Dorothea.

Dorann An invented name compounded of Dora and Ann.

Doreen, Dorene Variant pet forms of Dorothy and its diminutive Dora.

Doretta A diminutive form of Dora.

Dorie A variant form of Doris.

Dorinda   An eighteenth-century invented name styled after Belinda and Melinda. Rinda is a pet form.

Doris   From the Greek, meaning "a sacrificial knife."

Dorit   From the Hebrew *dor*, meaning "a generation."

Dorma   From the Latin *dormire*, meaning "to sleep," and the Old French *dormeour*, meaning "a window in a sloping roof."

Dorothea   The original form of Dorothy. From the Greek *doron*, meaning "gift," plus *theos*, meaning "God," hence "gift of God."

Dorothee   A variant form of Dorothy.

Dorothy   From the Greek *doron*, meaning "gift of God."

Dorri, Dorrie   Pet forms of Dorothy.

Dot, Dottie, Dotty   Pet forms of Dorothy.

Dova, Dove   From the Middle English *douve*, meaning "a dove."

Drusilla   A form of the Roman family name Drausus and its diminutive form Drusus.

Dulcie   From the Latin, meaning "charming, sweet."

Durene   From the Latin *durare*, meaning "enduring, lasting."

Dusty   A nickname. Dusty Deane was born in Texas during a raging dust storm.

Dyan   A variant form of Diana.

E

Eartha From the Old English, meaning "ground."

Ebony From the Greek, meaning "a hard, dark wood."

Eda A variant Italian form of Edda or Edith.

Eddy A masculine diminutive spelling of Eddie; a pet form of Edward. Also, from the Old Norse, meaning "a whirlpool."

Eden From the Hebrew, meaning "delight" or "adornment."

Edessa An ancient city in Mesopotamia, present-day Turkey.

Edie A popular Scottish diminutive form of Edith.

Edith, Edythe A compounded Anglo-Saxon name from *ead,* meaning "rich, happy, prosperous," and *gyth* or *guth,* meaning "battle, war."

Edna, Ednah From the Hebrew, meaning "delight, desired, adorned, voluptuous."

Edwina The feminine form of Edwin.

Edythe A variant spelling of Edith.

Effie A pet form of Euphemia, from the Greek, meaning "good speech," "well spoken."

Eileen An Irish form of Helen and Elaine.

Elaine French form of Helen, meaning "light" in the Greek.

Elana   From the Hebrew, meaning "a tree."

Elba   A variant form of Albert.

Elda   From the Middle English *elde,* meaning "old." Akin to Alda.

Ele   A pet form of Eleanor.

Eleanor, Eleanore   Variant German forms of Helen. From the Greek, meaning "light."

Electra   From the Greek, meaning "the shining one."

Elen   A variant spelling of Ellen. Also, a short form of Eleanor.

Elena   From the Greek, meaning "light."

Elenor   A variant spelling of Eleanor.

Elese   The Hawaiian form of Elsie.

Eliana, Eliane, Elianna   From the Hebrew, meaning "God has answered me." Akin to the masculine Elias and Elihu.

Elie   A pet form of Eleanor.

Elin   A variant spelling of Ellen. Also, a short form of Eleanor.

Elisa   A pet form of Elisabeth.

Elisabeta   The Hawaiian form of Elisabeth.

Elisabeth   A variant spelling of Elizabeth commonly used in England.

Elise   A pet form of Elisabeth.

Elissa A pet form of Elisabeth.

Elizabeth From the Hebrew, meaning "God's oath." Elisabeth (with an "s") is the way the Greek translation of the Bible rendered Elisheva, the original Hebrew form. It is the preferred spelling in Europe. Elizabeth, spelled with a "z", is the more common spelling.

Elke A pet form of Alice or Alexandra.

Ella A pet form of Eleanor.

Ellen A short form of Eleanor.

Ellyn, Elyn Variant spellings of Ellen and short forms of Eleanor.

Elma A variant spelling of Alma.

Elmira The feminine form of Elmer, from the Anglo-Saxon, meaning "noble and famous."

Eloise A variant form of the French Heloise and Louise.

Elsa A German diminutive form of Elizabeth. Or, from the Anglo-Saxon, meaning "a swan."

Else A variant spelling of Elsa.

Elsie A variant form of Elisabeth.

Elva From the Anglo-Saxon, meaning "elf."

Elysa, Elyse, Elyssa Variant forms of Elisabeth.

Elza From the Hebrew, meaning "God is my joy."

Ema The Hawaiian form of Emma.

Emaline   A variant form of Emily.

Emele   The Hawaiian form of Emily.

Emerald, Emeralda, Emeraldine   From the Middle English and the Old French *smaragde*, meaning "a bright green precious stone." Used also as a masculine form.

Emilia   A variant form of Emily.

Emilie   A variant form of Emily.

Emily   The feminine form of the Latin name Aemilius, meaning "ambitious, industrious."

Emma   From the Greek name Erma, meaning "the big one" or "grandmother."

Enid   Either from the Anglo-Saxon, meaning "fair," or from the Celtic, meaning "purity."

Erica, Erika   The feminine form of Eric. From the German, meaning "honorable ruler."

Erin   A poetic name for Ireland.

Erma   A variant spelling of Irma.

Erna   A feminine form of Ernest.

Ernesta   A feminine form of Ernest.

Ernestine   A feminine form of Ernest.

Errin   A variant spelling of Erin.

Esmeralda   From the Spanish, meaning "emerald."

Esther   From the Persian, meaning "a star."

Etana From the Hebrew, meaning "strong." Etan and Ethan are masculine forms.

Ethel From the Anglo-Saxon *aethel,* meaning "noble."

Eugenia From the Greek, meaning "well born."

Eugenie The French form of Eugenia.

Eunice From the Greek, meaning "good victory."

Eva, Eve Eva is the Latin and German form of Eve. Derived from the Hebrew, meaning "life."

Evangeline From the Greek, meaning "bearer of glad tidings, a messenger." A name created by Henry Wadsworth Longfellow.

Evanne An invented name, pronounced Eve-Anne.

Evelyn A variant spelling of the Celtic name Eveline, meaning "pleasant."

Evette A pet form of Evelyn.

Evie A pet form of Eve or Evelyn.

Evita A Spanish pet form of Eve.

Evona A variant form of Yvonne.

Evonne A pet form of Eva and Evelyn. Or, a variant form of Yvonne.

Evy A variant spelling of Evie.

𝓕

Fabia   From the Greek and Latin, meaning "bean farmer."

Faith   From the Middle English name Feith, and the earlier Latin *fidere*, meaning "to trust."

Falice, Falicia   Variant spellings of Felice.

Farrah   From the Arabic, meaning "a wild ass."

Fauna   The wife or sister of Faunus, who in Roman mythology is a god of nature, a patron of farming and animals.

Fawn, Fawna, Fawne   Either from the Middle English *faunen*, meaning "to be friendly," or from the Latin, meaning "a young deer."

Fay, Faye   From the Old French, meaning "fidelity," and often a short form of Faith.

Fedora   From the Greek, meaning "divine gift."

Felecia   A variant spelling of Felicia.

Felice, Felicia   From the Latin *felicitas*, meaning "happiness."

Feliciana   The Spanish form of Felicity.

Felicite   A French and Spanish form of Felicity.

Felicity   A variant spelling of Felice.

Fern   The feminine form of Ferdinand.

Fiona, Fione   From the Celtic, meaning "white."

Fleur   A French form of the Latin *flos*, meaning "flower."

Flora   From the Latin *flos* and *floris*, meaning "a flower."

Florence   From the Latin name Florentia, meaning "blooming."

Florenz   A German form of Florence.

Floria   A variant form of Flora.

Flower   A rare form of Flora and Florence first used in the seventeenth century.

Fortuna   In Roman mythology, the goddess of fortune.

Fortunata   From the Latin *fortuna*, meaning "chance, good luck."

Fran   A pet form of Frances.

Frances   The Old French feminine form of Franceis. From the French *franc*, meaning "free."

Francesca   An Italian form of Frances.

Francine   A pet form of Frances.

Françoise   A variant French form of Frances.

Frania   A variant form of Frances.

Freda   A variant form of Frieda.

Fredda, Freddie   Pet forms of Frederica.

Frederica   The feminine form of Frederic, meaning "peaceful ruler."

Frederika A variant spelling of Frederica.

Freida, Freide Variant forms of Frieda.

Freya In Norse mythology, the goddess of love and beauty.

Frieda From the Old High German, meaning "peace."

G

Gabi A pet form of Gabriela.

Gabriela, Gabriella From the Hebrew, meaning "God is my strength."

Gabrielle The French form of the Hebrew, meaning "God is my strength."

Gae A variant spelling of Gay.

Gail A pet form of Abigail.

Gainell From the Middle English *gainen*, meaning "to profit."

Gale A variant spelling of Gail.

Galia From the Hebrew *gaal*, meaning "God has redeemed."

Galya A variant spelling of Galia.

Ganya From the Hebrew, meaning "the garden of the Lord."

Gay From the Middle English *gai*, meaning "gay, merry."

Gayle A variant spelling of Gail.

Gemma From the Latin *gemma,* meaning "a swelling, a bud, a precious stone."

Gena A variant spelling of Gina.

Gene A pet form of Genevieve and Jean.

Geneva, Genevia From the Old French *genevre* and the Latin *juniperus,* meaning "juniper berry."

Genevieve From the Celtic, meaning "white wave."

Genie A pet form of Genevieve.

Genna A variant spelling of Jenna, a form of Jeanette.

Georgea A variant spelling of Georgia.

Georgeanne A name invented by combining George and Anne.

Georgette A pet form of Georgia.

Georgia From the Greek, meaning "husbandman, farmer."

Georgiana, Georgianna Pet forms of Georgia.

Georgina, Georgine Pet forms of Georgia.

Geraldene, Geraldine From the Old High German *ger,* meaning "spear," plus *hart,* meaning "hard."

Geralynne A name invented by combining Geraldine and Lynne.

Geri A pet form of Geraldine.

Germaine   From the Middle English *germain* and the Latin *germanus,* meaning "a sprout, a bud."

Gertrude   From the Old High German *ger,* meaning "spear," plus *trut,* meaning "dear," hence "adored warrior."

Gia   A pet form of Regina.

Gila, Gilah   From the Hebrew, meaning "joy."

Gilana   From the Hebrew, meaning "joy, exultation."

Gilda   From the Celtic, meaning "servant of God."

Gili   From the Hebrew, meaning "my joy."

Gilia, Giliah   From the Hebrew, meaning "my joy is in the Lord."

Gillian   A variant form of the Latin name Juliana, the feminine form of Julianus (Julian).

Gina   A pet form of Regina.

Ginette   A pet form of Virginia.

Ginger   A pet form of Virginia.

Ginnie, Ginny   Pet forms of Virginia.

Gipsy   A variant spelling of Gypsy.

Gisela, Giselle   From the Anglo-Saxon, meaning "a bright pledge" or "a sword."

Gizela   A variant spelling of Gisela.

Gladys   From the Welsh name Gwladys. A variant form of the Latin Claudia and the French Claude, meaning "lame."

Glenna   The feminine form of Glenn.

Gloria   From the Latin, meaning "glory."

Glory   A variant form of Gloria.

Glynis   From the British *glynn,* meaning "a glen, a narrow valley."

Golda   From the Old English and German, meaning "gold."

Goldie, Goldy   Pet forms of Golda.

Grace   From the Latin, meaning "grace." Gracie is a pet form. Grazia and Grazina are Italian forms.

Gracie   A pet form of Grace.

Grazia, Grazina   Italian forms of the Latin, meaning "grace."

Greta   A pet form of Margaret.

Gretchen   The German form of Margaret.

Guenevere, Guinevere   From the Celtic *gwen,* meaning "white wave" or "white phantom." In Arthurian legend, the wife of King Arthur.

Gussie, Gussy   Pet forms of Augusta.

Gwen   From the Celtic *gwen,* meaning "white."

Gwendaline   A pet form of Gwen.

Gwendoline   A pet form of Gwen.

Gwendolyn   A pet form of Gwen.

Gwenn, Gwenne   Variant forms of Gwen.

Gypsy   The name signifies "a bohemian" or "rover." Gipsy is a variant spelling.

ℋ

Hadassah   From the Hebrew, meaning "a myrtle tree," the symbol of victory.

Haley   From the Norse *haela*, meaning "a hero."

Halie, Hallie, Hally   Variant forms of Haley.

Hana   A variant spelling of Hannah.

Hania, Haniya   From the Hebrew, meaning "a rest place, an encampment." Hanniah is a variant spelling.

Hannah   From the Hebrew, meaning "gracious, merciful."

Hanniah   A variant spelling of Hania.

Happy   A nickname for a person with a happy disposition.

Harmony   From the Greek *harmonia*, meaning "a fitting, a blending into the whole."

Harriet, Harriette   Feminine forms of Harry, a variant form of Henry, an Old High German form of Heimerich, meaning "home ruler."

Harva   An invented name derived from Harvey.

Hasia   From the Hebrew, meaning "protected by the Lord."

Hasse   Possibly from the Old English *haesl*, meaning "a hazel tree."

Hattie, Hatty   Pet forms of Harriet.

Hava   From the Hebrew, meaning "life, alive."

Hayley   A variant spelling of Haley.

Hazel   From the Old English *haesl*, meaning "a hazel tree."

Heather   From the Middle English *haddyr*, meaning "a heath, a shrub, a plant."

Hedda   From the German, meaning "strife, warfare."

Hedia   From the Hebrew, meaning "the voice, the echo of the Lord."

Heidi   Probably a variant form of Hester and its pet form Hettie, both derivatives of Esther.

Helaine   A variant form of Helen, meaning "light" in the Greek.

Helen   From the Greek, meaning "a torch," hence "light."

Helena   A variant form of Helen.

Helene   The French form of Helen.

Henrietta   The feminine form of Henry. From the Old High German, meaning "home ruler."

Henriette   The French form of Henrietta.

Hermione   In Greek legend, the daughter of Menelaus and Helen of Troy.

Hester, Hesther   The Latin form of Esther.

Hestia   In Greek mythology, the goddess of the hearth.

Hila   From the Hebrew *hallel*, meaning "praise."

Hilary, Hillary   From the Latin *hilarius*, meaning "cheerful."

Hilda, Hilde   Variant forms of Hildegarde.

Hildegard, Hildegarde   From the German, meaning "battle protector, warrior."

Hildy   A variant form of Hildegarde.

Holli   A variant spelling of Holly.

Hollis   A variant form of Haley.

Holly, Hollye   From the Old English *holegn*, a variety of shrub with red berries, hung on the doors of ancient English homes to bring luck.

Holt   From the German *holz*, meaning "wood."

Honor, Honora   From the Latin, meaning "honorable."

Hope   From the Old English *hopa*, meaning "trust, faith."

I

Ianna   The feminine form of Ian.

Ida   From the Old English *ead* and *id*, meaning "a possession" and "protection," hence "a fortunate warrior."

Idana A name invented by combining Ida and Anna.

Idane From the Old German *id* and the Old Norse *idh*, meaning "labor."

Idena A name invented by combining Ida and Dena (Dinah).

Idette A pet form of Ida.

Ignacia, Ignatia Feminine forms of Ignatius.

Ilene A variant form of Eileen.

Ilisa, Ilise Variant forms of Elisabeth.

Ilka A Scottish form of the Middle English *ilke*, meaning "of the same class."

Ilsa A variant form of Elisabeth.

Ilyse A variant form of Elisabeth.

Imma From the Hebrew, meaning "mother."

Imogen, Imogene From the Latin, meaning "image, likeness."

Indi, Indy From the Hindi, meaning "Indian" or "from India."

Inez The Spanish form of Agnes.

Inga, Inge From the Old English *ing*, meaning "a meadow."

Inger A variant form of Inga.

Ingrid A variant Scandinavian form of Inga.

Iona   From the Greek, meaning "a purple-colored jewel."

Irena   A Polish form of Irene.

Irene   From the Greek, meaning "peace." Renie is a pet form.

Iris   From the Greek, meaning "a play of colors." In Greek mythology, the goddess of the rainbow.

Irma   From the Old High German Irmin, the name associated with Tiu, the god of war. A contracted form of Irmonberta and Irmgard.

Isa   A pet form of Isabel used chiefly in Scotland.

Isabel   A variant form of Elisabeth.

Isabella   The Spanish form of Isabel.

Isadora, Isidora   Variant forms of the masculine Isador.

Isolde   Probably from the Old High German, meaning "to rule."

Ivette   A variant form of Yvette.

Ivy   From the Middle English *ivi*, meaning "a vine (of the ginseng family)."

Jacklyn   A variant form of Jacqueline.

Jacoba   From the Hebrew, meaning "to supplant" or "protect."

Jacqueline, Jacquelyn, Jacquelynne   Variant French forms of Jacoba.

Jada From the Middle English and Old Norse *jalda,* meaning "a horse," especially an old, worn-out (jaded) one.

Jael From the Hebrew, meaning "mountain goat" or "to ascend."

Jaimie A feminine pet form of James.

Jalene A name invented by combining the masculine James and a variant form of Lenore (Eleanor).

Jamese A French feminine form of James.

Jan A pet form of Jeanette.

Jane From the Hebrew, meaning "gracious, merciful."

Janel, Janella, Janelle Pet forms of Jane.

Janet, Janette Pet forms of Jane.

Jani A pet form of Jane.

Janice A variant form of Jane.

Janis A variant form of Johanna.

Janita A variant form of the Spanish name Juanita, a pet form of Jane.

Janna A variant form of Johanna.

Jaqualine A variant spelling of Jacqueline.

Jara A Slavonic form of Gertrude.

Jaredene A feminine form of Jared. From the Hebrew, meaning "to descend."

Jasmin   From the Arabic and Persian *yasamin*, "a flower" in the olive family. Yasmin is the Persian form.

Jean, Jeane   Scottish forms of Jane.

Jeanette   A French form of Jane.

Jeanice   A variant form of Jean.

Jeanine   A pet form of Jane.

Jeanne   A variant form of Jane.

Jeannette   A French form of Jane.

Jeannine   A pet form of Jane.

Jemina   From the Hebrew, meaning "right-handed."

Jenise   A variant form of Janis.

Jennelle   An invented name. A combination of Jenny and Nell.

Jennie, Jenny   Pet forms of Jane.

Jennifer   From the Welsh name Guinevere which later became Winifred. Jen and Jenny are pet forms.

Jennilee   A name created by combining Jennifer and Lee.

Jeri, Jerri   A diminutive form of Geraldene.

Jerrilyn   A name created by combining Jerri and Lyn.

Jerusha   From the Hebrew, meaning "taken possession of, inheritance."

Jessica   A variant form of Jessie.

Jessie   From the Hebrew, meaning "God's grace," akin to Hannah.

Jetta   From the Old French *jaiet* and the Latin *gagates*, meaning "a hard variety of black coal which takes a high polish," hence the expression "black like jet."

Jewel, Jewell   From the Old French, meaning "joy."

Jill   A variant form of Gill (Gillian), meaning "girl."

Jinny   A Scottish form of Jenny.

Joan, Joann   Variant forms of Jane and Johanna.

Joanna, Joanne   From the Hebrew, meaning "God is gracious."

Jo-Ann, Jo-Anne   A hybrid name of Jo (Josephine) and Ann(e).

Jocelin, Joceline   A variant Germanic form of the Hebrew name Jacoba, the feminine form of Jacob, meaning "supplanted, substituted."

Jocelyn   A variant form of Jocelin.

Jodi, Jodie   Feminine pet forms of Judah, from the Hebrew, meaning "praise."

Jody   A variant spelling of Jodi.

Joelle   A feminine form of Joel.

Johanna   From the Hebrew, meaning "God is gracious."

Johnna   A variant spelling of Johanna or a feminine form of John.

Joia   An early form of Joy and Joyce (thirteenth century).

Joice   A variant spelling of Joyce.

Jolaine   An invented name. A combination of Joseph and Elaine.

Jolande   A variant spelling of Yolande.

Jolea   A name invented by combining Joseph and Lea.

Jolie   A French form of the Middle English *Joli*, meaning "high spirits, good humor, pleasant."

Joliet   A variant form of Juliet or Jolie.

Jona   A feminine form of Jonah.

Jorel   A name invented by combining Joyce and the masculine Reuel.

Josceline   An Old French form of Joceline.

Joscelyn   A variant spelling of Josceline, an Old French form of Jocelin.

Josepha   From the Hebrew, meaning "He (God) will add."

Josephine   A feminine French form of Joseph.

Josette   A pet form of Josephine or Jocelyn.

Josie   A pet form of Josephine or Joceline.

Joslyn   A variant spelling of Jocelin.

Joy   A pet form of Joyce.

Joya   A variant form of Joy.

Joyce   From the Latin *jocosa*, meaning "merry."

Joycelyn   A name created by combining Joyce and Lynne.

Juanita   A Spanish pet form of Juana (Jane).

Judith   From the Hebrew, meaning "praise."

Judy   A pet form of Judith.

Judyann   A name invented by combining Judy and Ann.

Julia, Julian, Juliana   From the Greek, meaning "soft-haired," symbolizing youth. Feminine forms of Julius.

Julie   A variant form of Julia.

Juliet, Juliette   French pet forms of Julia.

Julinda   A name invented by combining Julie and Linda.

June   From the Latin name Junius, meaning "the sixth month of the year." Akin to the masculine Junius.

Justina, Justine   From the Latin, meaning "just, honest."

K

Kacy   A name invented from the initials K.C.

Kaela   An invented name. Formed from Kathy (Katherine) and Ella.

Kandi   A variant spelling of Candy, a pet form of Candace.

Kara   A pet form of Katherine.

Kareen   A variant spelling of Karen.

Karen   A Danish form of Katherine.

Karin   A variant form of Karen.

Karina   A variant spelling of Carina, from the Latin, meaning "a keel."

Karita   A variant spelling of Carita.

Karla   A feminine form of Karl.

Karlene   A pet form of Karla.

Karmel, Karmela, Karmelit   From the Hebrew, meaning "vineyard." Karmel is also used as a masculine name.

Karmia   From the Hebrew, meaning "vineyard of the Lord."

Karna, Karnit   From the Hebrew *keren*, meaning "horn (of an animal)."

Karole   A variant spelling of Carole.

Karyn   A variant spelling of Karen.

Kasia, Kassia   Variant Polish forms of Katherine.

Kate   A pet form of Katherine.

Katharina, Katharine   Variants of Catherine.

Katherine   From the Greek *katharos*, meaning "pure, unsullied." Catherine is the more popular spelling.

Kathie, Kathy   Pet forms of Katherine.

Kathleen   An Irish form of Catherine.

Kati, Katie   Pet forms of Katherine.

Katrina, Katrine, Katrinka   Variant forms of Katherine popular in Slavic countries.

Katy   A pet form of Katherine.

Kay   From the Greek, meaning "rejoice." Also, a form of Katherine.

Kayla   A variant form of Kelila, from the Hebrew, meaning "a crown, a laurel."

Kelli   A variant spelling of Kelly.

Kelly   A variant form of Kelt (also spelled Celt). The Kelts were antecedents of the Gaelic families of Europe.

Kemba   From the Old English name Cymaere, meaning "a Saxon lord."

Kendy   An invented name. The feminine form of Kenneth.

Keren, Keryn From the Hebrew, meaning "horn (of an animal)."

Kerrie, Kerry From the British name Ceri, one of the early kings of Britain.

Kim An invented name made up of the first letters of Kansas, Illinois, and Missouri; these states meet at one point. A pet form of Kimberly.

Kimberly A name adopted from kimberlite, a type of rock formation often containing diamonds.

Kinsey Probably a variant form of Kin, from the Old English *cynn* and the Old Norse *kyn,* meaning "to produce," hence "offspring, relatives."

Kirby From the Old English *ciric,* meaning "a church."

Kireen From the Old English *ciric,* meaning "a church."

Kirsten From the Old English *ciric,* meaning "church," plus *stan,* meaning "stone," hence "stone church."

Kit, Kitty Pet forms of Katherine.

Kolleen A variant spelling of Colleen.

Krist, Krista Short forms of Kristin, a variant form of Christine.

Kristian A variant form of Christine.

Kristie A pet form of Christine.

Kristy A pet form of Kristin.

Kyla Variant form of Kayla.

Kyle   A variant form of Kyla.

Kyrene   From the Greek *kyrios*, meaning "a lord" or "god."

ℒ

Laila   From the Hebrew, meaning "night."

Lana   From the Latin *lanatus*, meaning "wooly." Also, a pet form of Alana.

Lanai   From the Hawaiian, meaning "a veranda, a terrace."

Lancey   A feminine form of Lance.

Lani   From the Hawaiian, meaning "sky."

Lara   A variant spelling of Laura.

Laraine   From the Latin, meaning "sea-bird."

Larisa, Larissa   From the Latin, meaning "cheerful."

Laura   From the Latin *laurus*, meaning "laurel." Akin to Laurel.

Laurel   From the Latin *laurus*, meaning "a laurel (tree)," symbol of victory.

Lauren, Laurene   Variant forms of Laura.

Laurette, Lauretta   Pet forms of Laura.

Lauri   A pet form of Laura.

Laurie   A pet form of Laura.

Laverne   From the Latin and French, meaning "spring, springlike; to be verdant."

Lavinia   From the Latin, meaning "woman of Rome."

Lawrie   A feminine form of Lawrence. Akin to Laura.

Lea   A variant French form of Leah.

Leah   From the Hebrew, meaning "to be weary."

Leala   From the Middle English *lele* and the Latin *legalis*, meaning "legal, loyal."

Leana, Leanne   Variant forms of Liana.

Leandra   A name invented by combining Lea and Ann.

Leanor, Leanore   Variant forms of Eleanor.

Leda   In Greek mythology, a Spartan queen, the mother of Helen of Troy.

Lee   From the Old English *lege*, meaning "meadowland."

Leeanna   A name invented by combining Lee and Anna.

Lei   A pet form of Leilani, from the Hawaiian, meaning "heavenly flower."

Leigh   From the Old English *lege*, meaning "meadowland." Akin to Lee.

Leila   From the Arabic and Hebrew, meaning "dark, oriental beauty" or "night."

Lela   A variant spelling of Leala.

Leland From the Old English *lege*, meaning "meadowland."

Lena A pet form of Eleanor, Helen, and Magadalene.

Lenis From the Latin *lenitus*, meaning "gentle, mild."

Lenora, Lenore Pet forms of Eleanor.

Leona From the Greek, meaning "lion-like."

Leora, Leorit From the Hebrew, meaning "light, my light."

Lera Possibly a variant form of the French *le roi*, meaning "the king."

Leron, Lerone From the Hebrew *lee rone*, meaning "song is mine."

Lesley, Leslie From the Old English *lege*, meaning "meadowlands."

Leta A pet form of Elizabeth.

Letitia From the Latin *laetita*, meaning "joy."

Letty A pet form of Elizabeth.

Levana From the Hebrew, meaning "the moon" or "white."

Levani From the Fijian, meaning "anointed with oil."

Levia From the Hebrew, meaning "to join."

Levona From the Hebrew, meaning "spice, incense," usually white in color.

Lexi   A pet form of Alexandra.

Lia   The Italian form of Leah.

Liala   Origin unknown.

Liana   From the French *lierne* and *liorne,* meaning "to bind, to wrap around."

Libbie, Libby   Pet forms of Elizabeth.

Liberty   From the Latin *libertas,* meaning "free."

Licia   A pet form of Alicia (Alice).

Lida, Lidia   Variant spellings of Leda.

Lila   A variant form of Lilac.

Lilac   From the Arabic and Persian *lilak,* meaning "bluish."

Lilian   From the Latin *lilium,* meaning "a lily." Or, from the Hebrew Elizabeth, meaning "God's oath."

Lilias   A variant form of Lilian.

Lilith   From the Assyrian and Babylonian, meaning "of the night." In ancient Semitic folklore, "a female demon"; the first wife of Adam before the creation of Eve.

Lillian   A variant spelling of Lilian.

Lily, Lilly   Pet forms of Lilian.

Lin   A variant spelling of Lynn.

Lina   A pet form of Carolina.

Linda   A pet form of Belinda.

Linde   A variant spelling of Linda.

Lindi   A pet form of Linda.

Lindsay, Lindsey   From the Old English, meaning "the camp near the stream."

Lindy   A pet form of Linda.

Linnet, Linnette   From the Old French *lin*, meaning "flax."

Lisa, Lise   Pet forms of Elisabeth.

Lisette   A pet form of Elisabeth.

Livia, Liviya   Pet forms of Olivia.

Liza   A pet form of Elizabeth.

Lizbeth   A short form of Elizabeth.

Lois   From the Greek, meaning "good, desirable."

Lola   A pet form of the Spanish Carlota (Caroline).

Loleta, Lolita   Pet forms of Lola.

Lora   From the Latin, meaning "she who weeps; sorrowful." Or, from the Old High German, meaning "famous warrior."

Loren   From the Latin, meaning "crowned with laurel."

Loretta   A pet form of Laura.

Lori   A pet form of Laura.

Loris   From the Dutch *loeres*, meaning "a clown."

Lorna   From the Middle English, meaning "alone."

Lorraine   A variant form of Lora.

Lotte   A pet form of Charlotte.

Louisa   An English form of Louise.

Louise   A feminine French form of Louis.

Louvenia   A name invented by combining the masculine Louis and a form of Lavinia.

Luana   From the Hawaiian, meaning "to be at leisure."

Lucia, Luciana   From the latin *lucere*, meaning "to shine."

Lucile, Lucille   From the Latin *lucere*, meaning "to shine, to bring light."

Lucinda   An English form of Lucia.

Lucy   An English form of Lucia.

Luisa   An Italian and Spanish form of Louise.

Luise   A variant French form of Louise.

Lyda, Lydda, Lydia   From the Greek place-name, meaning "a maiden from Lydia," an ancient kingdom in Asia Minor.

Lynn, Lynne   Variant spellings of Lyn.

M

Mackenzie   A Gaelic patronymic form, meaning "a son (descendant) of Kenneth."

Madelaine   A variant form of Magdalene.

Madeleine   A French form of Magdalene. Madlin and Maudlin are short forms.

Madeline   A variant form of Magdalene.

Mady   A pet form of Magdalene.

Mae   A variant spelling of May.

Magda   A German pet form of Magdalene.

Magdalen   A variant spelling of Magdalene.

Magdalene, Magdaline   From the Hebrew *migdal*, meaning "a high tower."

Maggie   A pet form of Margaret.

Mahalia   A variant form of Mahala, from the Aramaic and Arabic, meaning "fat" or "marrow, brain," or Mahola, from the Hebrew *mahol*, meaning "dance."

Maia   In Greek mythology, the daughter of Atlas, the mother of Hermes.

Majesta   From the Latin *majestas*, meaning "dignity, sovereign power."

Malinda   A short form of Marcelinda.

Mamie   A pet form of Mary or Margaret.

Manda A pet form of Amanda.

Mandy A pet form of Amanda.

Manette The pet form of the French name Marion.

Manuela A Spanish feminine form of Manuel.

Mara, Marah From the Hebrew, meaning "bitter."

Maralou A name invented by combining Mary and Lou.

Maralyn A variant spelling of Marilyn.

Marcelinda A variant form of Marcella.

Marcella From the Latin, meaning "brave, martial" or "a hammer."

Marcia A variant form of Marcella.

Marcie A variant form of Marcella and Marcia.

Marcy A pet form of Marcia.

Mardi A pet form of Martha. Used also as an independent name.

Maren, Marena From the Latin, meaning "sea." Akin to Marina.

Margaret From the Greek name Margaron, meaning "a pearl."

Marge A pet form of Margaret.

Margery A variant form of Margaret.

Marget A pet form of Margaret.

Margherita An Italian form of Margaret.

Margo, Margot Variant forms of Margaret.

Marguerita A Spanish form of Marguerite.

Marguerite From the French, meaning "a pearl, a daisy."

Maria The Latin, French, Italian, Spanish, and Swedish form of Mary.

Mariah A variant form of Maria.

Marian, Mariane, Marianne Variant forms compounded of Mary and Ann.

Maribeth A name invented by combining Mary and Beth.

Marie The French and Old German form of Mary.

Mariel, Mariele Dutch forms of Mary.

Marika A Slavonic pet form of Mary.

Marilee A name invented by combining a form of Mary and Lee.

Marilu A variant spelling of Marylu.

Marilyn, Marilynn Names derived from Mary and meaning "Mary's line" or "descendants of Mary."

Marina, Marinna From the Latin *marinus* and *mare*, meaning "the sea." Rina is a pet form.

Marion A pet form of the French name Marie. Also, a variant form of Mary.

Marisa   A variant form of Maris, from the Latin *mare*, meaning "the sea."

Marissa   A variant form of Maris.

Marjorie   In Scotland, the popular spelling of Margery.

Marla   A variant form of Marlene.

Marleen   A Slavic form of Magdalene.

Marlena, Marlene   Variant forms of Magdalene.

Marlo   A variant form of Marlene.

Marlowe   A variant form of Marlene.

Marna   A variant form of Marina.

Marsha, Marshe   Variant forms of Marcia.

Marta   A variant form of Martha.

Martha   From the Aramaic, meaning either "sorrowful" or "a lady."

Marthe   A French form of Martha.

Martina   A feminine form of Martin.

Martine   A feminine form of Martin.

Mary   The English form of the Greek names Mariam and Mariamne, derived from the Hebrew name Miriam, meaning "sea of bitterness, sorrow."

Marya   A Russian and Polish form of Mary.

Maryanne   A compounded name.

Marybeth   A hybrid form of Mary and Beth.

Marylin, Maryline Variant forms of Mary, meaning "from Mary's line" or "descendants of Mary."

Marylu A hybrid name of Mary and Lu (Louise).

Matilda A variant form of Mathilda, from the Old High German *macht,* meaning "might, power," plus *hiltia,* meaning "battle," hence "powerful in battle."

Matti, Mattie Pet forms of Mathilda.

Maud, Maude Pet forms of Mathilda.

Maura A variant form of Mary used predominately in Ireland.

Maureen A variant form of Mary.

Maurine A variant spelling of Maureen.

Mavis From the Old French *mauvis,* meaning "song thrush."

Maxime, Maxine Variant feminine forms of Maximilian.

May A pet form of Mary and Margaret.

Maya A variant spelling of Maia.

Mazana An invented name. A modification of the word "amazing."

Meg A pet form of Margaret.

Megan A variant form of Margiad, the Welsh form of Margaret.

Mehalia A variant spelling of Mahalia.

Mehira   From the Hebrew *mahir*, meaning "speedy, energetic."

Melane   A name invented by combining the masculine Mel and a form of the feminine Annis.

Melanie   From the Greek *melas*, meaning "black, dark in appearance."

Melicent   A variant form of Millicent.

Melina   From the Greek *melos*, meaning "a song."

Melinda   A variant spelling of Malinda.

Melissa   From the Greek, meaning "a bee," derived from *meli*, meaning "honey."

Melody, Melodye   From the Greek *melos*, meaning "a melody, a song."

Menora, Menorah   From the Hebrew, meaning "a candelabrum."

Mercedes   A variant form of Mercy.

Mercy   From the Latin *merces*, meaning "reward, payment," and in Late Latin "pity, favor."

Meredith   From the Welsh *mor*, meaning "sea," hence "protector of the sea." Used also as a masculine name.

Merie   A variant spelling of Merrie, from the Anglo-Saxon, meaning "joyous, pleasant."

Meris   A variant spelling of Maris.

Merit, Merritt   From the Latin *meritus*, meaning "deserving, having value."

Merla   A variant form of Merle.

Merle From the Latin and French, meaning "a bird" (blackbird).

Merlon From the Italian *merlo*, meaning "a battlement, a parapet."

Merril, Merrill Variant spellings of Meryl.

Merry From the Anglo-Saxon, meaning "joyous, pleasant."

Merryl A variant spelling of Meryl.

Meryl, Meryle Variant forms of Muriel or Merle.

Mia A short form of Hebrew name Michaela, meaning "Who is like God?"

Michel, Michele, Michelle French forms of Michal, a contracted form of the Hebrew, meaning "Who is like God?"

Midge A variant form of Madge, a pet form of Margaret.

Mildred From the Old English *milde*, meaning "mild," plus *thryth*, meaning "power, strength." Mil, Millie, and Milly are pet forms.

Milena From the Old High German *milo*, meaning "mild, peaceful."

Millicent From the Old French name Melisent and the Old High German name Amalswind, a form of *amal*, meaning "work," and *swind*, meaning "strong."

Millie, Milly Pet forms of Millicent and Mildred.

Mim, Mimi Pet forms of Miriam.

Mina   A pet form of Wilhelmina, a form of the masculine William.

Mindy   A pet form of Melinda and Mildred.

Minnie   A pet form of Miriam.

Mira   A short form of Miriam and Miranda.

Miranda   From the Latin *mirandus*, meaning "strange, wonderful."

Mirella   A short form of Mirabella, from the Latin, meaning "of great beauty."

Miriam   From the Hebrew *mar yam*, meaning "sea of bitterness, sorrow."

Mirra   A variant spelling of Mira.

Missie   A modern American name, meaning "young girl."

Misty   From the Old English *mistig*, meaning "obscure, covered with mist."

Mitzi   A pet form of Mary.

Moira, Moirae   In Greek mythology, the goddess of destiny and fate.

Mollie, Molly, Mollye   Pet forms of Miriam and Mary.

Mona   From the Irish *muadhnait*, meaning "noble."

Monette   A French pet form of Monday, from the Old English *monandaeg*, meaning "moon's day."

Monica   A variant form of Mona.

Moniece An invented name designed to sound like Denise, but to begin with an "m" so as to match the names of the other members of the family.

Monique A French form of Monica.

Morgan From the Welsh, meaning "sea dweller."

Morna From the Middle English *morne*, a form of the German *morgen*, meaning "morning."

Morrisa The feminine form of Morris.

Moyna From the Celtic, meaning "gentle, soft."

Muriel From the Irish *muir*, meaning "sea," plus *geal*, meaning "bright."

Musette From the Old French *muser*, meaning "to play music."

Myra A variant form of the Irish name Moira.

Myrna From the Greek and Arabic, meaning "myrrh," hence the connotation of bitter and sorrowful.

N

Nada, Nadia From the Slavic, meaning "hope," or from the Spanish, meaning "nothing."

Nadine A French form of the Russian *nadezhda*, meaning "hope."

Naia, Naiad From the Greek *naein*, meaning "to flow."

Nalani From the Hawaiian, meaning "calmness of the heavens."

Nan, Nana   Pet forms of Nancy, Ann, Anna, and Hannah.

Nancy   A variant form of Hannah, derived from the Hebrew, meaning "gracious."

Nanette   A pet form of Anna and Hannah.

Nani   From the Hawaiian, meaning "glory, splendor."

Naomi   From the Hebrew, meaning "beautiful, pleasant, delightful."

Nara   From the Celtic, meaning "happy."

Nastasya   A Russian form of Anastasia.

Natala, Natalia   Variant Russian forms of Natalie.

Natalie   A French and German form of the Latin *natalis*, meaning "to be born."

Natalya   A variant form of Natalie.

Natasha   A Russian pet form of Natalia (Natalie).

Nava, Navit   From the Hebrew, meaning "beautiful, pleasant."

Nayer   From the Persian, meaning "sunshine."

Neala   An Irish feminine form of Neal.

Neda, Nedda   From the British *naid*, meaning "a sanctuary, a retreat."

Nelda   An invented name. Meaning unknown.

Nellwyn   From the Old English, meaning "friend (*wyn*) of Nell."

Nelly   A pet form of Eleanor.

Nena   A variant spelling of Nina.

Neoma   Possibly from the Greek *nemos*, meaning "a wooded pasture."

Nerita   From the Greek *nerites*, meaning "a sea snail."

Nessa   From the Old Norse *nes*, meaning "a promontory, a headland."

Neta, Netta   From the Hebrew, meaning "a plant, a shrub."

Netania, Netanya, Nethania   From the Hebrew, meaning "gift of God."

Neva   From the Spanish, meaning "snow."

Nicci   The Italian form of the Latin *nike*, meaning "victory." Akin to the masculine Nicholas.

Nicola, Nicole, Nicolle, Nicolette   Feminine French forms of Nicholas.

Nika   A Russian feminine form of Nicholas.

Nila   A name adopted from the river Nile.

Nina   A French and Russian pet form of Anne (from Nanine).

Nirel   From the Hebrew, meaning either "a cultivated field" or "light of God."

Nissa   From the Hebrew *nes*, meaning "a sign, an emblem."

Nixie   From the Old High German *nihhus*, meaning "a water sprite."

Noel, Noelle   More commonly used as masculine names.

Noelani   The name of an Hawaiian princess, meaning "beautiful one from heaven."

Nola   From the Celtic, meaning "famous."

Nona   From the Laine *nonus*, meaning "the ninth."

Nora, Norah   Irish pet forms of Honora, Eleanor, and Leonora.

Noreen   A variant Irish form of Nora.

Norma   From the Latin, meaning "exact to the pattern; normal, peaceful."

Nova, Novia   From the Latin *nova*, meaning "new."

Noya   From the Hebrew, meaning "beautiful, or-namented."

Nureen   Possibly from the Hebrew *nur*, meaning "light." Also, a variant form of Noreen.

Nyla   A variant spelling of Nila, the name of an ancient Egyptian princess.

Nysa, Nyssa   From the Greek, meaning "the goal."

Octavia   From the Latin *octava*, meaning "the eighth."

Odele   From the Greek, meaning "an ode, a mel-ody."

Odelia   A variant form of Odele.

Odessa   From the Greek, meaning "of *The Odyssey*," referring to the ancient Greek epic ascribed to Homer.

Odetta, Odette   Pet forms of Odele.

Ofra   From the Hebrew, meaning "a kid, a young goat."

Olga   A Russian name, derived from Old Norse Helga, meaning "holy."

Olive, Olivia   From the Latin *oliva*, meaning "olive, olive tree," the symbol of peace.

Oma   A Sioux Indian tribal name, meaning "river people."

Oneida   From the Iroquois tribal language, meaning "standing rock."

Oona   An Irish form of the Latin *una*, meaning "one."

Opal   From the Sanskrit *upala*, meaning "a jewel."

Ophelia   From the Greek, meaning "to help."

Ora   From the Hebrew, meaning "light."

Oralee   From the Hebrew, meaning "my light" or "I have light."

Oria, Oriana   From the Latin *oriens*, meaning "Orient, the East."

Oriel   From the Old French *oriol* and the Latin *aurum*, meaning "gold."

Orlean, Orleans   A French form of the Latin *aurum*, meaning "gold."

Orli   From the Hebrew, meaning "light is mine."

Orma   A pet form of Ormanda.

Ormanda   A variant feminine form of Armand.

Ottalie, Ottilie   Variant Swedish forms of Otto.

Ova   From the Latin *ovum*, meaning "egg."

Page   From the Italian *paggio*, meaning "a boy attendant."

Pamela   A name coined by Sir Philip Sidney for a character in his novel *Arcadia* (1590).

Pandora   From the Greek *pan*, meaning "all, totally," plus *doron*, meaning "gift," hence "very gifted."

Pat   A pet form of Patricia.

Patia   A variant form of Patricia.

Patience   From the Latin *pati*, meaning "to suffer."

Patrice   A variant form of Patricia.

Patricia   From the Latin *patricius*, meaning "a patrician" or "one of noble descent."

Patsy   A pet form of Patricia.

Patti, Patty   Pet forms of Patricia.

Paula   From the Latin *paulus,* meaning "small."

Paulette   A pet form of Paula.

Paulina, Pauline   Pet forms of Paula.

Paz, Pazia, Pazit   From the Hebrew *paz,* meaning "gold." Paz is also used as a masculine name.

Pearl   From the Middle English *perle,* meaning "pearl."

Peg, Peggie, Peggy   Pet forms of Margaret and Pearl.

Penelope   From the Greek, meaning "a worker in cloth, a weaver" or "silent worker."

Penina, Peninah, Peninit   From the Hebrew, meaning "coral, pearl." Penny is a pet form.

Penny   A pet form of Penelope.

Peony   From the Greek Paion, an epithet of Apollo, physician of the gods. A flower of the buttercup family with medicinal properties.

Perri, Perry   Variant pet forms of Perrin.

Perrin, Perrine   Variant forms of the masculine Peter.

Persia   Probably from the Assyrian, meaning "to divide, to hinder."

Petite   From the French, meaning "small."

Petra   From the Greek, meaning "a rock."

Petrina   A Russian form of the Greek Petra.

Petronella, Petronilla   Variant forms of Petra.

Petula   From the Latin, meaning "impatient."

Petunia   From the French *petun*, referring to plants of the nightshade variety, with flowers of various colors and patterns.

Phebe   A variant spelling of Phoebe.

Phedre   From the Greek, meaning "the shining one."

Phemia   From the Greek *pheme*, meaning "voice, speech."

Phila   From the Greek, meaning "love."

Philana   From the Greek, meaning "lover of mankind."

Philippa   From the Greek, meaning "lover of horses."

Phillippa   A variant spelling of Philippa.

Phoebe   From the Greek, meaning "bright, shining one."

Phyllis   From the Greek *phyllon*, meaning "a leaf."

Pia   From the Latin, meaning "pious."

Pier   Probably a feminine form of Pierre, the French form of Peter.

Pilar   From the Latin *pilare*, meaning "a pillar, a column."

Plennie   From the Latin *plenus*, meaning "full, complete."

Polly   A variant form of Molly, which was often used as a pet name for Mary.

Pomona   From the Latin *pomum*, meaning "apple, fruit."

Poppy   From the Latin *papaver*, "a plant that yields a juice from which opium is made."

Portia   From the Latin *porcus*, meaning "a hog."

Prima   From the Latin *primus*, meaning "first, the best."

Priscilla   From the Latin *priscus*, meaning "ancient, old."

Q

Quanda   From the Old English *cwen*, meaning "a companion" or "a queen."

Queenie   From the Old English *cwen*, meaning "a queen."

Quinn   From the Old English *cwen*, meaning "a queen."

Quinta, Quintilla, Quintina   From the Latin, meaning "the fifth."

R

Rachel   From the Hebrew, meaning "a ewe, a female sheep."

Radella   A French form of the German *radi*, meaning "counsel."

Rae   A pet form of Rachel.

Raina   From the Latin *regnum*, meaning "to rule." Akin to Regina.

Raisa, Raissa   From the Yiddish, meaning "a rose."

Raizel, Rayzel, Razil   Pet forms of Raisa.

Ramona   A short form of the masculine Raymond.

Randa   A feminine form of Randall.

Randi   A pet form of Randa.

Rane   A variant form of Raina.

Rani   From the Hebrew, meaning "my joy."

Ranit, Ranita   From the Hebrew, meaning "joy" or "song."

Raphaela   The femine form of Raphael.

Raquel   A variant Spanish form of Rachel.

Ray, Raye   Variant spellings of Rae.

Raya   From the Hebrew, meaning "friend."

Razi   From the Aramaic, meaning "my secret."

Razia, Raziah, Raziela   From the Aramaic, meaning "secret of the Lord."

Rebecca   From the Hebrew and Arabic, meaning "to tie, to bind."

Regan   A variant form of Regina.

Regina   From the Latin *regnum*, meaning "to rule," hence "queen."

Reida   A variant form of Rita.

Reina, Reine   Variant forms of Raina.

Rena, Reena   Pet forms of Regina or Serena.

Renana, Renanit   From the Hebrew, meaning "joy, song."

Rene, Renee   French forms of Renata, meaning "to be born again."

Renette   A French pet form of Rene.

Renita   A Spanish pet form of Rene.

Retha   A short form of Marguerita.

Reubena, Reuvena   Feminine form of Reuben.

Rhea   From the Greek, meaning "protector of cities" or "a poppy" (flower).

Rhoda, Rhode   From the Greek, meaning "a flower" (rose).

Rhona   A hybrid of Rose and Anna.

Rhonda, Rhondda   From the Celtic, meaning "powerful river."

Ria   From the Spanish, meaning "a small river."

Richia   A feminine form of Richard.

Ricki   A pet form of Ricarda, a feminine Italian form of Richard.

Ricky   A variant spelling of Ricki.

Riesa   A pet form of Theresa.

Rilla From the Dutch *ril* and Low German *rille,* meaning "a little stream."

Rimona From the Hebrew, meaning "a pomegranate."

Rina A variant spelling of Rena.

Rishona From the Hebrew, meaning "first."

Rita From the Sanskrit, meaning "brave" or "honest."

Riva From the Old French *rive* and the Latin *ripa,* meaning "a bank, coast, shore."

Rivka The Hebrew form of Rebecca.

Roanne A hybrid of Rose and Anne.

Robbie A pet form of Roberta.

Roberta The feminine form of Robert.

Robin A pet form of Roberta.

Robyn A variant spelling of Robin.

Rochella A variant form of Rochelle.

Rochelle From the Old French *roche,* meaning "a large stone."

Rohana A hybrid of Rose and Hannah.

Rolanda A feminine form of Roland.

Rolene A feminine form of Roland.

Roma The Italian form of Rome, named for Romulus.

Romaine   A variant form of Roma.

Romelda, Romilda   From the German, meaning "Roman warrior."

Romy   A variant form of Roma.

Rona   From the Gaelic *roman,* meaning "a seal."

Ronda   A variant spelling of Rhonda.

Ronee   A feminine pet form of the masculine Ronald.

Roni   From the Hebrew, meaning "my joy."

Ronia   From the Hebrew, meaning "my joy is in the Lord."

Ronna   A feminine variant form of Ronald.

Ronnie   A feminine pet form of Ronald.

Rori, Rory   Irish feminine forms of Roderick and Robert.

Rosa   The Italian form of Rosa.

Rosabel   From the Latin and French, meaning "beautiful rose."

Rosabeth   A hybrid of Rosa and Beth.

Rosalia, Rozalia   From the Latin *rosalia,* pertaining to the ceremony of hanging garlands of roses on tombs.

Rosalind   From the Latin, meaning "beautiful rose."

Rosalyn   A variant form of Rosalind.

Rose   The English form of the Latin *rosa*, meaning "any genus of shrub of the rose family."

Roseanne   A hybrid of Rose and Anne.

Rosedale   From the Old English, meaning "a valley of roses."

Roselyn   A variant form of Rosalind.

Rosemary   A hybrid of Rose and Mary.

Rosetta   An Italian pet form of Rose.

Rosette   A French pet form of Rose.

Roslyn   A variant spelling of Rosalyn.

Rowan   From the Old English *ruh*, meaning "rugged land."

Rowena   A variant form of Rowan.

Roxane, Roxanna, Roxanne   From the Persian, meaning "dawn, brilliant light."

Royce   More commonly used as a masculine name.

Roz   A pet form of Roslyn.

Rozanne   A variant spelling of Roseanne.

Ruby   From the Latin *rubeus*, meaning "red, reddish."

Rue   From the Old High German *hruod*, meaning "fame."

Rula   From the Middle English *reule* and the Latin *regula*, meaning "ruler."

Runa From the Old Norse *rinna*, meaning "to flow, to cause to run."

Ruth From the Hebrew and Syriac, meaning "a companion; friendship."

S

Sabina A variant form of Sabine.

Sabine From the Latin, meaning "of the Sabines," an ancient Italian people who conquered Rome in 290 B.C.

Sabra From the Hebrew, meaning "thorny cactus."

Sabrina A pet form of Sabra.

Sacha A pet form of Alexandra.

Sada A variant form of Sadie.

Sadi A variant spelling of Sadie.

Sadie A pet form of Sarah.

Sadira From the Arabic, meaning "an ostrich returning from water."

Salena, Salina From the Latin *sal*, meaning "salt."

Sallie, Sally Variant forms of Sarah.

Samantha From the Aramaic, meaning "the listener."

Samara From the Latin *samara* and *samera*, meaning "the seed of the elm."

Samira From the Arabic, meaning "entertainer."

Sande, Sandi Pet forms of Sandra.

Sandra A pet form of Alexandra.

Santina From the Latin *sancta*, meaning "little saint."

Sara A modern spelling of Sarah.

Sarah From the Hebrew, meaning "princess, noble."

Sarai The original biblical form of Sarah.

Saretta A pet form of Sarah.

Sari From the Hindi and Sanskrit, meaning "an outer garment worn by Hindu women."

Sarina, Sarine Variant forms of Sarah.

Sarita A Spanish form of Sarah.

Saundra A variant spelling of Sandra.

Savina A variant form of Sabina.

Scarlet, Scarlett From the Middle English, meaning "a deep red color."

Sela From the Hebrew, meaning "a rock."

Selda From the Old English *seldan*, meaning "strange, rare, precious."

Selena A variant form of Selene.

Selene From the Greek, meaning "the moon."

Selina A variant spelling of Selene.

Selma From the Celtic, meaning "fair."

Serena From the Latin *serenus*, meaning "peace-ful."

Shana A variant spelling of Shaina, from the Yiddish, meaning "beautiful."

Shane, Shanie Variant spellings of Shaina.

Shannon A feminine variant form of Sean.

Shari A pet form of Sharon.

Sharleen, Sharlene Variant spellings of Charlene.

Sharon From the Hebrew *yashar*, meaning "a plain, a flat area."

Sharyn A variant spelling of Sharon.

Sheba A pet form of Bathsheba.

Sheena, Shena Gaelic forms of Jane.

Sheila, Sheilah, Sheilla Variant forms of Cecelia and Celia introduced into Ireland by early settlers.

Shelia A variant form of Sheila.

Shelley, Shelly Irish pet forms of Cecelia.

Sheree A variant form of Cheryl.

Sherelle, Sherrelle Variant spellings of Cheryl.

Sheri A variant form of Cheri.

Sherran A variant form of Sharon.

Sherrie A variant spelling of Sheri.

Sherry   A variant pet form of Cheryl.

Sheryl, Sheryle   Variant forms of Cheryl.

Shiela, Shielah   Variant spellings of Sheila.

Shira, Shirah   From the Hebrew, meaning "song."

Shiri   From the Hebrew, meaning "my song."

Shirley   From the Old English *scire*, meaning "a shire, a district," plus *lea*, meaning "a meadow," hence "the meadow where the district meetings were held."

Sibil, Sibilla   Variant forms of Sibyl.

Sibyl   From the Greek *sibylla*, meaning "sorceress, fortune teller," women considered prophets by ancient Greeks and Romans.

Sid   A pet form of Sidney.

Sidne   A variant spelling of Sidney.

Sidney   A contracted form of Saint Denys. Commonly used as a masculine name.

Simone   A French form of Simon.

Sirena   A variant spelling of Serena.

Sisley   A variant spelling of Cicely.

Sissie, Sissy   Pet forms of Cecelia.

Sivia, Sivya   From the Hebrew *tzvi*, meaning "a deer."

Sofia   An Italian form of Sophia.

Sondra   A variant spelling of Sandra.

Sonia, Sonja, Sonya   Variant Slavic and Russian forms of Sophia.

Sophia   An English and German name from the Greek *sophos* and *sophia*, meaning "wisdom, skill."

Sophie   The French form of Sophia.

Sparkle   From the Middle English *sparklen*, meaning "to throw off sparks, brighten."

Spring   From the German *springen*, meaning "to leap."

Stacey, Stacy   Irish forms of Anastasia.

Stacia, Stacie   Pet forms of Anastasia.

Star   From the Old English *steorra*, meaning "a star."

Starr   A variant spelling of Star.

Stefana, Stefania   Variant forms of Stephanie.

Stefanie, Stefenie   Variant spellings of Stephanie.

Stella   From the Latin, meaning "star."

Stephanie, Stephenie   From the Greek *stephanos*, meaning "a crown."

Suanne   A hybrid name of Sue (Susan) and Anne.

Sue   A pet form of Susan.

Suella   A hybrid of Sue (Susan) and Ella.

Susan   From the Hebrew *shoshana,* meaning "a rose" or "a lily."

Susanna, Susannah   Variant forms of Susan.

Susanne   A variant form of Susan.

Suzanne   A variant spelling of Susanne.

Sybil   A variant spelling of Sibyl.

Sybille   A variant form of Sibyl.

Sylvia   From the Latin *silvanus,* meaning "forest."

T

Tabitha   From the Greek and Aramaic, meaning "a roe, a gazelle."

Talia   From the Hebrew, meaning "dew."

Talma, Talmit   From the Hebrew, meaning "mound, hill."

Talor, Talora   From the Hebrew, meaning "dew of the morning."

Tamanique   A name invented by adding a French ending to a form of Tammy.

Tamar   From the Hebrew, meaning "a date-yielding palm tree."

Tamara, Tamarah   Variant forms of Tamar.

Tamath   A variant form of the Arabic *tamasha,* meaning "to walk around."

Tami, Tammy   Feminine forms of Thomas. Also, pet forms of Tamar.

Tana   A variant form of Dana.

Tania   From the Russian, meaning "the fairy queen."

Tanith   From the Old Irish *tan*, meaning "an estate."

Tanya   A variant spelling of Tania.

Tara   Either a French name derived from the Arabic, meaning "a measurement," or from the Aramaic, meaning "to throw" or "to carry."

Taryn   Probably a variant form of Tara.

Tasha   A short form of Natasha.

Tate   From the Anglo-Saxon, meaning "to be cheerful."

Tatum   A variant form of Tate.

Tauba   From the German *taube*, meaning "a dove."

Tavi   A variant form of the masculine form David.

Tavita   A pet form of Tavi.

Taylor   An Anglo-Saxon occupational name, meaning "a tailor." Used also as a masculine name.

Teresa   The Spanish and Italian form of Theresa.

Teri   A pet form of Theresa.

Terranda   From the Latin *terra*, meaning "earth," plus *andr*, meaning "man," hence "man's earth."

Terry   A pet form of Theresa.

Tess, Tessie   Pet forms of Theresa.

Thalia   From the Greek, meaning "to flourish, to bloom."

Thea   A short form of Althea.

Thelma   From the Greek, meaning "a nursling, infant."

Theodora   The feminine form of Theodore.

Theresa   From the Greek *therizein,* meaning "to reap."

Therese   The French form of Theresa.

Tiffany   A variant form of the Latin *trinitas,* meaning "three, the trinity."

Timora   From the Hebrew *tamar,* meaning "tall," as the palm (tamar) tree.

Timothea   From the Greek, meaning "honoring God."

Tina   A pet form of names ending in "tina," such as Christina and Bettina.

Tira   From the Hebrew, meaning "encampment, enclosure."

Tobi   A variant spelling of Toby.

Toby   A variant form of Tova, from the Hebrew, meaning "good."

Tova, Tovah   From the Hebrew, meaning "good." Toba is a variant spelling.

Toyah   From the Scottish *toy,* a woman's headdress with flaps that hang over the shoulder.

Tracey, Tracy   From the Anglo-Saxon, meaning "brave."

Tricia   A pet form of Patricia.

Trina   A short form of Katrina, a form of Katherine.

Trish, Trisha   Short forms of Patricia.

Trudi, Trudy   Popular pet forms of Gertrude.

Tuesday   From the Old English *tiwesdaeg*, meaning "tiu's day."

Tyna   A variant form of Tyne.

Tyne   From the British *tain*, meaning "a river."

U

Ualani   From the Hawaiian, meaning "heavenly rain."

Unity   From the Latin *unus*, meaning "one."

Urania   From the Greek *ouranos*, meaning "heaven."

Ursa   From the Latin, meaning "a she-bear."

Ursala   A variant spelling of Ursula.

Ursula   A pet form of the Latin *ursa*, meaning "a she-bear."

Uta   Probably from the Spanish tribal name Yutta, meaning "mountain dwellers."

$\mathcal{V}$

Val   A pet form of Valerie and Valentine.

Valari   A variant form of Valerie.

Valencia   From the Latin, meaning "strong, vigorous."

Valentia   A variant spelling of Valencia.

Valentina   An Italian form of Valentine.

Valentine   From the Latin *valens,* meaning "healthy, strong."

Valeria   From the Latin *valere,* meaning "to be strong."

Valerie   A French form of the Latin name Valeria, meaning "to be strong."

Vanessa   From the Greek, meaning "a butterfly."

Vanora   From the Celtic, meaning "white wave."

Venetia   From the Latin, meaning "a woman of Venice."

Venus   From the Latin, meaning "to love."

Vera   From the Latin *vera* and *verus,* meaning "truth."

Verity   From the Latin *veritas,* meaning "truth."

Verna   From the Latin *veritas,* meaning "truth."

Verne, Vernee   From the Latin, meaning "green, springlike."

Vernique   A French form of Verne.

Vernona   A variant form of Verne.

Veronica   From the Latin *veritas*, meaning "truth." Akin to Verity.

Vici, Vicki, Vicky   Pet forms of Victoria.

Victoria   From the Latin, meaning "victorious."

Vikki, Vikkie   Pet forms of Victoria.

Vincentia   From the Latin *vincere*, meaning "to conquer."

Viola   From the Middle English and Latin, meaning "a violet."

Violet   The Old French form of Viola.

Violeta, Violetta   Italian pet forms of Violet.

Virginia   From the Latin *virginitas*, meaning "virgin, pure" or "a maiden."

Vita   From the Latin, meaning "life, animated."

Vivian, Viviana   From the Latin *vivus*, meaning "alive."

Vivien, Vivienne   French forms of Vivian.

Wanaka   The Hawaiian form of Wanda.

Wanda   A Middle English form of the Old Norse *vondr* and the Gothic *wandus*, meaning "a slender, supple shoot; a young tree."

Wandis A variant form of Wanda.

Wanika The Hawaiian form of Juanita.

Wannetta, Wanette From the Old English *wann*, meaning "young pale one."

Warrene The feminine form of Warren.

Wasida From the Old English *waes*, meaning "water."

Welthy, Welty From the Old English *wolcen*, meaning "a cloud," and later, "the sky."

Wenda From the British *gwen*, meaning "fair."

Wendey, Wendi, Wendy Pet forms of Gwendaline and Wenda.

Wenona, Wenonah From the Old English *wen*, a variant form of *win*, meaning "joy, bliss." Also, an American Indian name, meaning "firstborn daughter."

Wilda From the Old English *wil*, meaning "a willow."

Wilenda A name invented by combining William and Brenda.

Willa A pet form of Wilhelmina, a feminine form of William.

Willeta, Willetta, Willette Feminine forms of William.

Wilmet, Wilmette Pet forms of Wilhelmina, a feminine form of William.

Winifred From the Old English, meaning "friend of peace."

Winnie   A pet form of Winifred.

Winona   A variant spelling of Wenona.

Wyn   A pet form of Gwendaline and Winifred.

Wyome   From the Algonquin Indian language, meaning "large plain."

X

Xena   A variant form of Xenia.

Xenia   From the Greek *xenia,* meaning "hospitality," and *xenos,* meaning "a guest, a stranger" (to whom hospitality was extended).

Ximena   A variant form of Xenia.

Y

Yardena   The feminine Hebraic name for Jordan.

Yeira   From the Hebrew *or,* meaning "light."

Yemina   From the Hebrew, meaning "right hand."

Yetta   A pet form of Henrietta.

Yolanda, Yolande   Possibly, a form of the Old French name Violante, which is a derivative of Viola.

Yosefa, Yosifa   Variant spellings of Josepha, the feminine form of Joseph.

Yvette   A variant French feminine form of Yves.

Yvonne   A variant French feminine form of Yves.

Zabrina   A variant form of Sabrina.

Zaida   From the Yiddish, meaning "grandfather."

Zamora   A variant form of Zimra, from the Hebrew *zemer*, meaning either "a branch" or "song of praise."

Zandra   A variant form of Sandra.

Zara, Zarah   Variant forms of Sarah.

Zeena   A variant spelling of Zina, a variant form of Zinnia.

Zelda   A variant form of Selda.

Zelia   From the Latin *zelus*, meaning "zealous."

Zelma   A name invented by combining parts of Zaida, Ella, and Mark.

Zemira, Zemora   From the Hebrew, meaning "a branch."

Zena   A short form of the Persian *zan*, meaning "a woman."

Zenia   A variant form of Zena.

Zia   From the Hebrew, meaning "to tremble."

Zinnia   A variety of plant with colorful flowers, named for German botanist J.G. Zinn (died 1759). Zeena, and Zina are variant forms.

Ziona   From the Hebrew, meaning "excellent" or "a sign."

Feminine Names

Zoe　From the Greek, meaning "life."

Zonya　A variant form of Sonia.

Zophia　A variant form of Sophia.